ATLA

OCEAN

DURAS

NICARAGUA

Pan American Highway

○Managua

The War
of the Dispossessed

The WAR of the DISPOSSESSED

Honduras and El Salvador, 1969

Thomas P. Anderson

University of Nebraska Press • Lincoln and London

Library of Congress Cataloging in Publication Data

Anderson, Thomas P   1934–
The war of the dispossessed.

Bibliography: p. 189
Includes index.   1. Salvador-Honduras Conflict, 1969.   I. Title.
F1488.A5   972.83'052   80–24080
ISBN 0–8032–1009–4

To
Leonel Gómez Vides,
without whose friendship and aid
this book would have been impossible

Contents

Maps

Preface

The origin of this work lies in the fact that I was in El Salvador, writing a study of the 1932 uprising, when the 1969 war with Honduras broke out. Having connections with the Salvadorean army, I was invited to go into occupied Honduras as an "observer." This memorable experience impressed upon me the suffering of the poor folk caught up in this disaster, Hondurans and Salvadoreans alike. I began to see that neither side was blameless in bringing about the war, nor was there any one villain one could point to as being responsible.

Although I resolved in 1969 that I would write on the war, it was some time before the opportunity arose. The research began in 1977 and went on through the summer of 1979. I was delighted with the open and friendly response which I met in the foreign ministries of both countries. The archives, including many classified documents never before used in any study of the war, were opened to me. In both ministries I was provided with a private room in which to work and plied with such attentions as endless cups of coffee and even an occasional sandwich. Despite the earnest desire of both sides to be of assistance, I soon discovered the difficulty of archival research in Central America. Hardly any of the documents had been cataloged, and few were bound. The trivial and the important were heaped together, making it necessary to plow through great masses of paper. This is not said as a reproach to either ministry nor to excuse any errors, for which I take total responsibility. Their budgets are small and their staff few, and they are, of course, much more concerned with the day-to-day workings of diplomacy than with what some researcher might want to find out about past events.

Therefore I should like to express my thanks to Pablo Pineda Madrid and his staff in Tegucigalpa, and to Arturo Castrillo Hidalgo and his staff in San Salvador, as well as to Chancellor José Antonio Rodríguez Porth of El Salvador and Vice-chancellor Policarpo Callejas of Honduras, who gave their permissions for this research. I would also like to thank all those who allowed me to talk to them about the subject of this book. Some of them are listed at the end of the bibliography.

Getting funding for this research proved to be very difficult, and that in part accounts for the long delay in beginning the work. Therefore I should like to express my gratitude to the Eastern Connecticut State College Foundation for its generous help, as well as to certain private individuals in Central America who came forward with aid and hospitality. I should like to add my appreciation of the tremendous assistance of Mrs. Blanche Blum, who typed the manuscript.

Especially I should like to thank Fidel Chávez Mena and also those friends who opened to me the hospitality of their homes, René Herrera and Jeanette Noltenius. I should also like to thank don René's niece, Margarita Herrera, for her constant solicitude about my welfare, and most of all, the person to whom I owe so much and to whom this book is dedicated, Leonel Gómez Vides.

The War
of the Dispossessed

Chapter 1
Central American Unity: A Dream Deferred

On 14 July, 1969, "the day of French national liberation," as they like to remind people in El Salvador, at 5:50 P.M., there was an angry roar of internal combustion engines in the sky over the capital city of San Salvador. At that moment I was taping an interview with Señor Joaquín Castro Canizales on the history of his country. We looked, saw nothing, and went on talking. A few minutes later air-raid sirens went off across the city, and at 6:30 the electricity and water both disappeared. Still, no one knew whether it was a drill, an attempted coup, or an attack until 7:30 when a battery-powered receiver picked up an announcement from Radio Guatemala that the territory of Honduras had just been bombed. The roar that shattered the calm of that fine July evening had been the Salvadorean air force making a surprise attack on Toncontín Airport outside Tegucigalpa, and on airports at San Pedro Sula, Santa Rosa, and several other locations.

That surprise attack led to a war which officially lasted only four days—hence the popular name for it, "The Hundred-Hours War,"—but which in reality went on much longer. In the course of these hostilities, perhaps as many as two thousand people were killed, twice that number wounded, a hundred thousand refugees created, fifty million dollars lost, and the dream of Central American unity again shattered.[1] Here then was an event of considerable importance not only for the two desperately poor countries who engaged in the combat but for all of Central America.

The causes of the conflict are difficult to disentangle amid the welter of charges and countercharges that have come from the contending powers. At the time of the war, the North Amer-

1

ican press played it up as "the Fútbol War," for it followed the series of three soccer contests between El Salvador and Honduras in the Central American section of the World Cup competition. These matches, the first in Honduras and the second in El Salvador, led to a good deal of rowdyism and even violence, so that the third game had to be transferred to Mexico City. But if there is one thing that all sensitive observers agree on, it is that the war was not over something as trivial as football.[2] Indeed, the squabbles during the games were the product of existing tensions, not the source of the hostility.

A more sophisticated approach suggests that population pressures in El Salvador were at the root of the problem. Certainly these pressures were very real. By 1970 this tiny and backward country had a population density of 470 persons per square mile. It is no wonder therefore that some three hundred thousand Salvadoreans had migrated to relatively underpopulated Honduras. But this study will attempt to show that population pressure in El Salvador was only one of a number of complex factors leading to the war of 1969. Hondurans who are knowledgeable about the affair like to point to the very real internal problems of El Salvador, both in economics and politics, as being basic to the conflict. But Honduras also had profound economic, political, and social problems within its boundaries, which will be explored in considerable detail. Ultimately I hope to demonstrate that the key to this tragic conflict lay in the thousands of simple peasants on both sides of the border, peasants like those throughout Central America, dispossessed by arrogant oligarchies linked to military dictatorships.

But in order to begin, the conflict must be put within the framework of Central America itself, for an understanding of this framework is essential to the story. As General Fidel Sánchez Hernández, president of El Salvador at the time of the war, remarked in an interview with me, "All wars in Central America are essentially civil wars." This feeling of kinship within the Central American community is very strong and has deep historic roots. Under the Spanish empire there existed an entity called the Kingdom of Guatemala, governed from the city of the same name by a captain-general. It comprised six provinces:

Chiapas, which is now in Mexico; Guatemala; San Salvador; Honduras; Nicaragua; and Costa Rica. Each of these had a governor subordinate to the captain-general, an arrangement which was confirmed by King Carlos III in 1786 and again by the Spanish Cortés in May 1821, just before independence.[3] However, since the captain-general was subordinate to the viceroy of New Spain in Mexico City, it was only natural that Mexico, upon achieving independence, should try to bring Central America into its new empire under the upstart Emperor Iturbide in 1822. But within a few months Iturbide's empire had ceased to exist, Mexico became a republic, and the general whom the emperor had sent to govern in Guatemala tactfully advised the Central Americans to make their own governmental arrangements. Thus was born the United Provinces of Central America. As so often after, the chief architect of unity was a Salvadorean, José Manuel Arce, who, along with his uncle, the priest José Matías Delgado, had led the first, abortive uprising against Spain in 1811.

Arce was not, however, the man to hold things together. Liberal, anticlerical elements accused him of selling out to the conservative aristocracy once he had installed himself in Guatemala City. They broke with him and found a leader in Francisco Morazán, the Honduran military leader who is a national hero in both Honduras and El Salvador. Morazán was a man of many talents, a soldier and leader as well as administrator.[4] Born near Tegucigalpa in the 1790s, he was in his mid thirties when he took over the ragged liberal forces of Honduras in 1827. By April of 1829, he had marched into Guatemala City and installed his fellow liberal José Francisco Barrundia as president. The new leaders of Central America then launched a series of anticlerical "reforms" so dear to the hearts of Spanish American liberals in the nineteenth century. Morazán became president of Central America in 1830.

Guatemala City remained a hotbed of clerical and aristocratic intrigue, and so Morazán decided to move the capital of Central America to the more sympathetic San Salvador in 1834. That was a mistake. Revolt soon broke out in Guatemala under the leadership of an Indian mule-skinner named Rafael Carrera, who was to become the darling of the clerical faction. The occa-

3

sion of this revolt was the widespread epidemic of Asiatic cholera which devastated the country in 1838–39 and which was blamed by many on liberal doctors who allegedly poisoned streams in order to kill off the pious Indian peasants and their priests. In the semimedieval world of Guatemala, such charges could be and were believed. Carrera, whipping his machete-wielding Indians into a frenzy, soon routed the liberals and established a personal dictatorship which would last until 1865.[5]

Morazán, in San Salvador, now found the Central American state disintegrating around him. Costa Rica, always wary of incorporation in a larger unit, seceded in April 1838. Nicaragua then declared herself "free, sovereign, and independent," followed by Honduras, which separated in early 1839 and joined Nicaragua in a military alliance. Morazán continued to rule in San Salvador, first declaring himself chief of that province and then marching on Guatemala City. The decisive battle between Carrera and Morazán took place there on 18 March 1840. On the first day of fighting, Morazán occupied the city, only to be driven out at four o'clock the next morning by the wily conservatives. Returning to El Salvador, he took a ship from the port of La Libertad for exile in Costa Rica. There Morazán made such a political nuisance of himself that he was taken out and shot in 1842.[6]

There followed for Central America what Mario Rodríguez calls "a violent period of ideological struggles and unadorned selfishness."[7] Each republic was forced to endure its growing pains: internal upheavals and external wars were frequent as each state sought its own advantage. From Guatemala, Carrera dominated the period, installing Francisco Malespín as his puppet president in El Salvador and meddling in the tangled affairs of Honduras. The liberals of the area rallied around Gerardo Barrios, who ousted the conservatives for a brief period in his native El Salvador. But an invading Guatemalan army deposed him; and when he tried a political comeback in Nicaragua, pro-Carrera forces captured him and sent him back to El Salvador, where he was executed in the same year that Carrera died.

Strangely enough, such a turbulent era did not lack attempts at reunification. In fact eight times between 1842 and

1862, two or more countries attempted to revive the dream of unity.[8] At Chinandega, Nicaragua, in March 1842, representatives of Honduras, El Salvador, and Nicaragua met together, although Guatemala and Costa Rica refused to attend. In July of that year, the three countries signed a pact of confederation, and a government was established in San Vicente, El Salvador, on 29 March 1844. This was designed to create a federal government with a president elected for a four-year term, but within a year the plan had fallen through. Meetings followed at Sonsonate and then at Nacaome, on the Honduras–El Salvador border, resulting in the Pact of Nacaome of October 1847. Unfortunately, this attempt to reestablish unity was ratified only by Honduras, El Salvador, and Nicaragua. Carrera disdained participation; and the Costa Ricans, although taking part in the discussions, never ratified the plan, which was thus stillborn.[9]

Despite the many failures, there were many pressures to continue negotiations. For Honduras there was continued trouble with the British, who had occupied the islands off the north coast and then the port of Trujillo in October 1849, in an effort to collect the debts owed to British bankers. All three of the middle countries feared too great a domination by Guatemala. Thus the representatives of El Salvador, Honduras, and Nicaragua met again in 1851 and formulated the National Representation of Central America, which was not exactly a government, but was designed to represent the republics before a hostile world. Carrera, however, disapproved and soon deposed the president of the Representation, José Francisco Barrundia. He then marched into Honduras and installed his own puppet, Santos Guardiola, as president in February 1856. Guardiola, known in Honduran history as "the Butcher," kept the situation on ice for some time.

However, the adventures of William Walker, a romantic Southern doctor who dreamed of creating a personal empire in Central America, soon pointed up the need for unity. In the middle of the 1850s, Commodore Vanderbilt and Daniel Drew were competing for control of the Nicaraguan route across the isthmus and on to California, where gold had been discovered. Backed by Drew, Walker overthrew the government of Nicaragua, only to be driven out after a protracted war in which Costa

Rica, Honduras, and El Salvador, bankrolled by the Commodore, aided the anti-Walker forces in Nicaragua. Walker later returned to Honduras and was shot by a firing squad. The rallying to defeat Walker, the so-called National War, marked a highpoint of joint Central American action. It was in the wake of the National War that Gerardo Barrios tried his hand at unification, forming a confederation of El Salvador and Honduras in 1862 with the object of overthrowing Carrera, which, as we have seen, resulted in Barrios's own exile and eventual death.

There was in all this a common pattern: El Salvador generally took the lead in the quest for unity, supported by the weaker Honduras. Nicaragua often joined in; but Guatemala, the strongest of the Central American states, and Costa Rica, with the least populace, tended to remain aloof.

It was another Barrios who next attempted the task of reuniting Central America: Justo Rufino Barrios, the liberal president of Guatemala from 1873 to 1885. Conditions appeared favorable. There was considerable sentiment in Honduras for a permanent union with El Salvador in 1871. Meetings had opened on an optimistic note at La Unión, El Salvador, early in 1872, with representatives of Guatemala, Honduras, and Costa Rica, as well as the host country. But the negotiations not only broke down, they resulted in an invasion and the overthrow of Honduras by Guatemala and El Salvador the following month. Shortly afterwards, Justo Rufino Barrios took over Guatemala as a liberal reformer. He proved an able administrator, a violent anticlerical, and a good drill master who built an army of Indian peasants. Like Carrera before him, he sought to extend his power beyond Guatemala, dreaming of a Central America united under his leadership. By force he installed his puppet, Rafael Zaldíivar, in El Salvador as a step toward unification; but Zaldíivar betrayed his master, and Barrios proclaimed a war of national unification for Central America. At the head of his army, he invaded El Salvador, only to be killed in the very first battle. His army melted away and with it Guatemala's dream of a forceful reunificaiton.[10]

Barrio's death dampened plans for union.[11] His successor, Manuel Lisandro Barrillas, convened a meeting of all five republics in Guatemala in January 1887; and several treaties resulted, which encouraged a second meeting at Managua in 1889. From Managua an Act of Union was promulgated, providing for gradual unification, but again, as so often in the past, a change of administration ruined all their plans. In this case it was the mysterious death of Salvadorean President Francisco Menéndez. His death led to a coup by General Carlos Ereta, who withdrew his country from the scheme.[12]

It was the turn of Honduras and Nicaragua to take the lead when in 1895 their presidents, Policarpo Bonilla and José Santos Zelaya, brought together representatives of their own states and El Salvador to create the Greater Republic of Central America, to which Guatemala and Costa Rica soon adhered. This Plan of Amapala did not propose a unified state, but rather a confederation with a five-man governing diet or junta, in which the executive power would be rotated. The diet would be chosen by the national legislatures. This scheme was wrecked by events in El Salvador, where General Tomás Regalado overthrew President Rafael Antonio Gutiérrez and withdrew from the Greater Republic in 1898.[13]

The following year an organization called the Partido Unionista Centroamericano was founded by Salvador Mendieta, a Nicaraguan visionary who, until his death in 1958, remained the Don Quixote of Central American unity. He pursued this goal endlessly and with great vigor through his organization, which was more of an intellectual movement than a genuine political party.[14]

In the early days of the present century, the United States began to conceive that its interests might best be served by ending Central American anarchy. The occasion for North American intervention was the war which broke out between Honduras and Nicaragua in 1907. The war began when a group of Hondurans attempted to overthrow their president, Manuel Bonilla. He squelched the revolt and promptly put the blame on President José Santos Zelaya, the long-term Nicaraguan strong man. A Honduran force invaded Nicaragua only to be repulsed. Zelaya now launched an attack on Honduras in March and, defeating Honduran forces and some Salvadorean volunteers, deposed Manual Bonilla. Theodore Roosevelt, considering the strong United States economic interests in both countries, then brought about a conference in Washington. The Central American Peace Conference began on 14 November 1907, and ended on 20 December, having created six major treaties. The most important of these was the one establishing the Central American Court. This court would have one judge from each of the Central American republics and would last ten years before renewal. To everyone's surprise all five republics quickly ratified the plan for this court of arbitration.[15]

For some years the court acted as a stabilizing influence in the region, but it was finally destroyed by the very country which had been instrumental in its creation, the United States. The problem was the Bryan-Chamorro treaty between the United States and Nicaragua, giving the former the right to build a canal across the latter and to fortify the Gulf of Fonseca. El Salvador and Costa Rica both claimed that their rights had been violated and took the case before the Central American Court, which ruled in their favor in 1917. The United States and Nicaragua ignored the ruling, and Nicaragua recalled its judge, which doomed the Court. The Court was not renewed in 1918.

Despite the frustrations of the Central American Court fiasco, El Salvador called a meeting in 1920 to work on the question of unity. Nicaragua, still touchy about the Bryan-Chamorro treaty, did not participate; but the remaining four states signed agreements covering a uniform law code, unification of their educational systems, lower tariffs, and a common currency. The Pact of Central American Union was signed on 19 January 1921.[16] But it was the same old story; the pact was never ratified, and a coup in Guatemala put an end to any hopes that it might be.

A generation later, in 1945, Juan José Arévalo, the idealistic Guatemalan president, and General Salvador Casteneda Castro, the Salvadorean strong man, planned a merger of their countries. They declared Santa Ana, a major city in El Salvador near the Guatemalan border, as the new capital. The citizens of Santa Ana had hardly time to celebrate their good fortune before this scheme, too, fell apart.

In the postwar period regional organizations proliferated throughout the world, and the Central Americans were not slow to see that they might achieve a degree of their long-sought unity by having their own. In October 1951 they met at San Salvador and established the Organización de Estados Centroamericanos (ODECA). A secretary-general, housed in a magnificent San Salvador mansion, was to do the day-to-day work of the organization, but regular meetings of the five foreign ministers were to be held along with the occasional "summits." Ratification was prompt, and the organization began its work on 14 December 1951. Its first secretary-general, elected for a four-year term, was José Guillermo Trabanino, a distinguished Salvadorean. At long last Central America appeared to have an organization with real life.

The existence of ODECA spurred the drive for economic integration. El Salvador set up a free-trade zone with Nicaragua in 1951; and in June 1958, meeting in Tegucigalpa, the five states signed a Multilateral Treaty of Free Commerce and Econimic Integration. They drew up a list of two hundred items that might be exchanged among the five duty free. It aimed at total free trade within twenty years. The Accord of San José, in September 1959, regulated those duties which remained; and the Treaty of Economic Association was signed in February of the next year. This last, however, ran into ratification problems, especially in Costa Rica. Ultimately, it was necessary for President John F. Kennedy of the United States to visit the country and intercede for the treaty.[17] Thus began the career of the Mercado Común Centroamericano (MCCA).

If Central America had not achieved political integration, it at least appeared to have created two organizations, ODECA and MCCA, which would help bring together the various countries of the region. But these hopes would be destroyed by the war of 1969. The headquarters of ODECA still stand in San Salvador, the lawn is well kept, the flags of the five nations fly from their staffs, but in reality the organization is impotent and moribund. The Central American Common Market too continues to enjoy a shadow existence, although no trade at all has gone on between El Salvador and Honduras since 1969.

This brief sketch of the pursuit of Central American unity has spanned a century and a half. It is a tangled story in which the names and events are familiar only to specialists in the affairs of the region. But the recounting of this history of frustration is designed to make an important point: the tenacity of the ideal of union; and the equal persistence of bitter rivalries, petty jealousies, and political chaos, which have made the ideal an unachievable one.

It would be well to note how often these rivalries have led to violent clashes between the Central American governments. Before 1969 the last serious shooting war had occurred in 1907 between Honduras and Nicaragua, but the tendency remained. Border clashes were frequent throughout the area; and in 1954 the United States Central Intelligence Agency used Honduran and Nicaraguan airfields in staging its overthrow of the government of Guatemala, while in 1957 there were violent clashes along the Honduran border with Nicaragua.

This long history of conflict forms an essential part of the background of the 1969 war. Hugh Thomas once remarked that the failure of outsiders to understand the Spanish Civil War of the 1930s lay in their inability to grasp the fact that it was really *another* Spanish civil war, and part of a long sequence of such events. It is the same in the present case. However, while the struggle of the last decade between El Salvador and Honduras must be understood in the light of all that had gone before in Central America, it would be a mistake to assume that this war was primarily about common markets or reunification efforts. The basis of this particular conflict must be sought in the relationship of man to the land within the two contending states—a relationship shaped in each case by forces peculiar to the time and place. That is why the reader is now asked to turn to the internal histories, first of El Salvador and then of Honduras. Without a grasp of the relationship between *campesino* and landholder, between soldier and civilian, between unionist and employer, the struggle appears as no more than so much sound and fury, or as an amusing comic opera called the Soccer War.

Chapter 2
El Salvador: Under the Volcanoes

There seems to be a rule in El Salvador that every major city must have its own volcano. Thus there is a volcano of San Salvador, one of Santa Ana (the nation's second largest city), and one for each of the two other major centers, San Miguel and San Vicente. These volcanoes are inactive, but then one never knows about volcanoes. Their existence is perhaps symbolic of the pent-up, always seething, ready to explode, but seldom actually exploding, social and political atmosphere of the country itself. El Salvador is a country that keeps the lid on, but just barely. The officer does not sleep soundly in his *cuartel,* nor the rich man in his castle, behind his stone walls with jagged glass scattered over the top. Everything, even the careful, tense way that people move on the street, seems to suggest a potential for massive violence. Occasionally something does snap, as it did in the great rising of 1932 and in the war of 1969, the two most important events in the history of modern El Salvador.

These tensions, which no doubt help give El Salvador one of the world's highest murder rates, originate in the social and economic conditions of the people. In particular the agricultural situation of the country is important for understanding its people since the country remains by and large agrarian. And to understand the agriculture, one must begin with the geography.

As countries go, El Salvador is not large. The total territory of the modern republic is something under eight thousand square miles (the exact figure is hard to arrive at for reasons that will become clear), making it roughly the size and shape of New Jersey. In addition to the volcanoes, there are many ranges of hills, often jagged and irregular. Between are fertile valleys, some narrow and deep, some broad and flat with great agricultural potential. As one nears the Pacific, which bounds the coun-

11

try to the south, the hills give way to a littoral plain which becomes increasingly broad toward the east.

The climate of this land shows two distinct seasons: the hot, wet period running from April to October is known as "the winter" although the country is north of the equator. The dry season, or "the summer," is actually cooler. During this latter period virtually no moisture falls; the hills become dry and barren. Great dust storms blow up and increase the erosive effects of the violent rains of the wet season. However, the average rainfall is not overly abundant (even in the rainy season it may go days, or even a week, without raining); but in general there is sufficient moisture to grow all but the most temperamental tropical plants.

(It is a land of great beauty, of breathtaking vistas and bright sunshine, of spectacular thunder storms and clear blue lakes. The Indians believed that the land was a goddess, and one of great fertility. It was one of the early centers of plant domestication. 1)

Before Columbus this goddess was shared by two distinct people whose domains roughly divided at the Lempa River, which runs through the country. In the mountainous west lived the Nahuati-speaking Pipil Indians, related to the Aztecs of Mexico. To the east lived Mayas. Both had a high degree of civilization and an organized agricultural life. For their subsistence they relied on maize, beans, squash, and other native crops, much as their mestizo descendants do today; but for their trade they relied on the sacred beverage chocolate. Cacao was traded far afield for such things as jade, obsidian, and precious metals.[2]

The Indian did not simply farm; he was intimately bound up in the agricultural process. Cacao was sacred, corn was a god, and ritual and magic surrounded every act of the vegetative cycle. No one owned the land. The local chiefs of the villages periodically redistributed it to the families on the basis of need. Public granaries insured that no one starved or, at least, that all starved equally.

Into this world, at once simple and complex, strode the *conquistadores* in 1524, led by the formidable Pedro de Alvarado. After bloody battles the Indian kingdoms were suppressed and the population made to fit into Spanish patterns of exploitation. The Indian villages were forced to pay a tribute, technically due to the crown, to the local Spanish landlords. This system, known as the *encomienda,* meant that the Indians in fact paid the *encomendero* through their labor on his estate. The *repartimiento,* or occasional forced drafts of labor, was also used. The *encomienda,* disliked equally by the crown and the Indians, was gradually transformed into a system of peonage by which Indians were induced to leave their native villages and transfer themselves to the haciendas of their Spanish masters. Here they were often given a *milpa,* or garden plot, and a house. In return they worked in the fields belonging to the hacienda. Through a process of making the peon increasingly indebted to his patron, the clever landowner could transform his peons into virtual slaves.

Finding neither gold nor silver, the Spaniards from the start relied on agriculture for their wealth, chiefly cultivating cacao and collecting so-called Peruvian balsam from the natives. These continued to be the chief cash crops throughout the sixteenth century until overproduction caused a decline in the market. The settlers then began to emphasize the production of indigo and the raising of cattle for their cash income. The *hacendados* allowed their cattle to stray freely across the land, to the despair of the Indian villagers who saw their corn and other food crops ravaged by the beasts. But cattle will not eat the indigo plants; and indigo, especially in the milling of the dye, required a considerable force of Indian labor, dragooned by *repartimiento.* These mills, with their crowded conditions and lack of sanitation, caused the death of a great many workers.[3]

The effects of Spanish farming methods upon the population were considerable. The Spaniards were never more than a small minority compared to the Indians. The latter were to some extent protected by the crown and the Church, both of which tried, futilely, to maintain the separate identity of Indian villages. But with crops destroyed by roving cattle, and under pressure from Spanish landlords more and more villages became absorbed into the nearby haciendas. The absolute numbers of the native population likewise began to decline to such a degree that not until the 1890s did the country regain its pre-Columbian populations, thanks to the diseases brought over by the settlers. As their traditional pattern of communal village farming began to disappear, more and more Indians found themselves landless, defrauded by the Spanish or, increasingly, by mestizos who could count on the cooperation of the law courts. Those Indians who did not become peons often ended up as titleless squatters, living precariously at the sufferance of the legal landholders.[4]

The coming of independence did little to aid the economy of the region. Indeed, it led to a loss of traditional markets with the result that much land which had been cultivated reverted to open pasutre, while with the loss of colonial prosperity, local fairs also declined. Frequent wars with Guatemala effectively cut off the country from Atlantic-coast ports and forced El Salvador to develop its own Pacific-coast ports of La Libertad and La Unión.[5]

Gradually, despite transportation problems, the economy began to recover from the shock of independence, with indigo, cattle, and sugar being the chief sources of wealth. But indigo began to drop on the world market as early as the 1870s, and by the end of the century, the indigo market was severely depressed.[6] The government, seeing this problem, began to encourage the search for a new export crop, giving tax exemptions to producers of rubber, coffee, tobacco, vanilla, and other cash crops. It was coffee that provided the solution.

In fact, not only did coffee provide the solution but coffee became king in El Salvador. Having been introduced around the time of the break with Spain, it had begun to expand rapidly in the 1860s. So sudden was the phenomenon that production in the Santa Ana region trebled in the years between 1877 and 1881. After that, growth was sporadic, but unstoppable. In 1915 the value of coffee exports was $7,372,000, which soared to the sum of $22,741,000 by 1928, making coffee by far the largest export crop in the country. By 1933 coffee covered 96,523 hectares out of the 286,545 in principal crops, or 33.7 per cent.[7]

Such a spectacular growth was bound to bring with it profound social and economic changes. To begin with, unlike indigo, which could be grown throughout the country, coffee required a highly specialized environment. It grew best on the slopes of the volcanoes and the higher hills throughout the land at two to four thousand feet above sea level. This restricted most of the production to the area from San Salvador westward to the Guatemalan border, although there was a large coffee area as well between San Vicente and San Miguel in the eastern highlands. Again, unlike indigo, which is a very accommodating plant, coffee requires a good deal of specialized care. Its bushes must be planted under shade trees to keep off the tropical sun; and the trees, like the bushes themselves, require tending and cultivation. Even today there is considerable debate among growers as to what type of tree is best for growing in conjunction with coffee. Once planted, the bushes take anywhere from three to five years to produce the fruit, which is harvested between October and February, depending on the altitude and climate. Once harvested, coffee requires as extensive a preparation as does indigo. The "cherries" must be taken to a *beneficio*, or mill, where they are washed under warm water, causing them to split and display the beans, which are milled to remove the thin outer husk. The beans must then be graded and shipped.[8] Thus coffee created a great demand for the choicest land and an abundance of cheap labor.

No one has pointed out better than Abel Cuenca, a Marxist scholar of modern El Salvador, the social effects of these demands. In his work *El Salvador: Una Democracia Cafetalera*, he indicates that coffee was at first a progressive force in the national economy. It did not introduce plantation life—indigo and sugar has long since done that—nor did it at first compete with these crops for land, as it needed its own specialized environment. But as prices increased, coffee *fincas* began to swell, moving even into marginal coffee lands in a vast effort to profit from the boom. One result of this was a decline in food crop production and soaring food prices during the 1920s.[9] It was the *hacendado* who would profit from coffee expansion, not the *campesino*, for the government and the lawyers were very much on the side of the former.

During the long centuries since conquest, much had already changed in the countryside. For one thing, there had been an amalgamation of Spanish and Indian racial types to produce

15

a mestizo people, known in Central America as *ladinos*. Until 1932 there were still a number of Indian communities, especially in the extreme western regions, but by and large a mixed race was predominant. As the distinction between Indian and white had become blurred, so had the distinction between the Indian towns and the municipalities of the settlers. By the coming of independence, most towns were governed in a uniform pattern, and almost all of them had the same sort of arrangements for dealing with lands owned by the municipal council. These lands were essentially of two types: the *tierras comunes*, which were "commons" in the British sense, free pasture and woodlot where the *vecinos*, the citizens of the *municipio*, might graze their stock; and the *ejidos*, lands which might be rented by the town in order to raise revenue. Under the Spanish system both of these might be very extensive.[10]

Coincident with the rise of the coffee economy in El Salvador, was the domination in that country of the doctrines of economic and political liberalism. These doctrines, borrowed from the writings of such thinkers as Adam Smith, Jeremy Bentham, and John Stuart Mill, held that in granting the individual maximum political and economic freedom lay the best possibility for stimulating progress. To those who thought in these terms, the role of the individual, as an economic as well as a political unit, was paramount; and any sort of corporate land ownership was seen as an inhibition of progress. These ideas had coincided nicely with the liberals' dislike of the Church, a great corporate landholder who could then be expropriated for the best progressive reasons. These reasons also caused the liberals to take a strong look at communal lands at the very moment when the coffee growers were seeking expansion. What could be more natural than to "rationalize" the pattern of land tenure in the country by doing away with communal lands? Gerardo Barrios, that unlucky patriot, had transferred government estates to coffee planters. His liberal successors resolved to go much further.

During the presidency of Rafael Zaldívar (1876–85), the matter came to a head. Zaldívar, a "pragmatic liberal," as Alastair White styles him,[11] ordered a survey of the common lands in 1879. This was seen as a prelude to their abolition; and those who were anxious to seize upon them had not long to wait, for on 26 February 1881 a decree came forth abolishing communal lands. A year later, on 2 March 1882, the *ejidos* were also abolished. Marco Virgilio Carías sees this as a critical step toward the situation which produced the war of 1969.[12]

What then happened was that coffee, according to Jorge Schlesinger, "opened a profound chasm in the Salvadorean collectivity."[13] The small farmer who had relied on the common pasture and woodland for part of his sustenance was forced into economic ruin. His land was taken from him by law, or by force and fraud, and a new class of wealthy *finca* owners became the elite of the country. Many who had fancied their tenancy on the *ejidos* to be permanent now found themselves squatters on their land, and although a law was passed in 1884 allowing those who bought up these lands to expel them, they clung tenaciously to the soil with the stubborn persistence of their Indian ancestors. Some of the rural poor continued in the role of *colonos*, that is, as peons who were given a place to live on the hacienda, or *finca*, and generally a garden plot, or *milpa*. They were to also receive a small salary, either in money or in kind. On the *latifundias* which grew sugar or indigo, there was a great need for some permanent force; but coffee is so seasonal that while a few families might be kept on in this role, for the most part the *finca* relied on occasional hired hands.[14] A survey of 1950 revealed that 19.2 per cent of land exploitations (or 33,398 out of 174,204) were on increasingly small plots, for the growing population made for constant subdivision. On the other hand, in 1960 it was estimated that .01 per cent of the large landholders owned 16 per cent of the land.[15]

Out of these arragements a pattern of life began to develop for the *campesinos*. Many of them might farm a small plot either as squatters, as small owners, or as *colonos*. But these plots were not sufficient for the sustenance of their families. Therefore they would follow the harvests, working the coffee *fincas* during the harvest season, then moving on to work cutting sugar cane or harvesting the cotton during August and September. Behind them they hoped, if they had not been evicted, that their corn was ripening on their *milpas*. The migratory nature of this life style caused a great deal of social havoc. Family life became impermanent and unstable. Many women in El Salvador lived along the roadsides among the coffee *fincas* of the west, in shacks of wattle and daub, in old cardboard cartons, in aluminum-roofed lean-tos. They waited for the men who came each year to work and who might support them for a time if they were lucky. Men came every year, but often not the same men, and they left pregnant women behind. Well over half the births in El Salvador were illegitimate.

As the rural poor sank into misery, an elite of wealth and power was developing. There had always been rich men in the country, owners of great haciendas of cattle, henequen, or sugar; but now the wealth became increasingly concentrated in the hands of the few. Before World War I, there had been about three hundred and fifty great agricultural properties, half of them outside the coffee area. The owners of these used the boom period after the war to buy up increasing amounts of land, especially for coffee.[16] An aristocracy of wealth began to transform itself into what Richard N. Adams calls the "cosmopolitan upper class."[17] El Salvador has long had a legend that it is ruled by *los catorce*, the fourteen families. This is a myth and not subject to documentation, but myths often tell us more than sober statistics. Salvadoreans instinctively feel the oppressive presence of such an elite; and if no one can agree on the actual family names of those who make up *los catorce*, certain names are identified over and again as members of the group: Dueñas, Regalado, Duke, Sol, Sandoval, Escalón, Meléndez.

Below the very rich international playboy set and the local aristocracy of such regional centers as Santa Ana, people whom Richard N. Adams refers to collectively as *la sociedad* or *gente de primera categoría*, there existed a small middle class. This included those who might own a few hectares of land, enough to support themselves decently. It included as well businessmen and shopkeepers, civil servants, and military officers. But this middle class was very small and, with the exception of the officer class, politically ineffective. There was also a small urban working class, with its struggling trade unions. In the early 1930s, when the capital city had only about eighty thousand inhabitants of the country's million and a half, 80 per cent of the population could have been classified as *campesinos*, or peasants.[18]

The life of the rural poor was, and is, difficult in the best of times. The onset of the great depression made it infinitely worse because the value of the *colon* fell from 2.04 to the dollar in 1929 to 2.54 to the dollar in 1932, while the national income by 1931 sank to 50 per cent of what it had been in 1928. The *campesinos* had been making about fifty *centavos* a day before the depression. Their wage now fell to twenty *centavos*. Fortunately, food prices also fell steeply after 1930, corn dropping to half its 1928 value by 1932, rice to about 75 per cent of its 1928 value, and beans to little more than half their predepression cost.[19]

As coffee was king, everything depended on the price of this commodity. It had risen consistently through the twenties; but even before the Great Crash, starting in July 1929, coffee prices in El Salvador began to ebb. From a price of thirty-two to thirty-seven *colones* per *quintal* in July (about the average for the previous year), the price fell to seventeen to twenty *colones* by the end of the year. After that the price continued downward.[20] In great alarm the growers formed the Asociación Cafetalera, in ¹December 1929, to look after their interests in the market. Unfortunately, this association was dominated by the great growers: the 350-odd growers out of 3,400 who owned 125 acres or more of coffee land. The result was that the small growers were forced out of business, ruined by the mighty who then bought up their lands.

It was at this point that the social volcano of El Salvador ceased to slumber. Peasant unrest was not a new phenomenon in the country. Often it had been tied to the resentment of the disappearing Indian community over the expropriation of their lands and their cultural impoverishment. In 1833 an Indian by the name of Anastasio Aquino of Santiago Nonualco, in the south-central part of the country, had risen up and massacred the nearby *ladinos*. Only with great difficulty was the revolt put down. In 1872, a decade before the wholesale expropriation of the *ejidos*, there was a revolt in the Pipil Indian village of Izalco in the western part of the country over a local expropriation of common lands. In the twentieth century harsh treatment, frauds by the overseers and by the company stores, and low wages, had led to economic desperation among the rural poor in the coffee districts, even before the bottom fell out of the coffee market.[21] This economic desperation had produced scattered revolts during the 1910s and 1920s put down by the Guardia Nacional, a tough paramilitary force modeled on the Spanish Guardia Civil, which had been founded in 1912.

As long as *campesino* revolt was isolated and uncoordinated, it posed little threat to the government; but starting in the early twenties, forces had been at work to give cohesion to the peasant masses and to turn them into a formidable opponent. Unions among urban workers and some of the peasantry had begun to form in 1922 with the organization of the Unión Obrera Salvadoreña, which merged in 1924 with the Confederación Obrera de El Salvador. These were fairly tame groups compared to the rival Federación Regional de Trabajadores de El Salvador, which was part of the Marxist Confederación Obrera Centroamericana. Through these groups a sense of class consciousness began to grow.

A small, clandestine communist party first appeared in 1925, and by 1930 it had surfaced as a force in the politics of the country. The guiding genius of the communist movement was Agustín Farabundo Martí, the son of a small coffee planter in the province of La Libertad, who had become at the university an outspoken opponent of the governing class. He was expelled from the country in February 1920, joined General Augusto César Sandino in his famous, though futile, campaign in Nicaragua, and reappeared in his native land in May of 1930.[22] He soon formed a group of bright and energetic young men, such as Alfonso Luna and Mario Zapata, both of whom would be executed along with him, and Abel Cuenca and Miguel Marmol, both of whom miraculously survived.[23] After a period of intensive preparation, this group began to lay plans for a revolt which would capitalize upon the discontented *campesinos* of the western part of the country, and in particular upon the Indians of the Izalco region.

Before going into the history of this revolt, which along with the 1969 war looms as one of the two great events of El

Salvador's history in the twentieth century, it might be wise to say a few words about the complex politics of the country. Following the death of Carrera in Guatemala, and of Gerardo Barrios in the same year, 1965, the liberals began to gain strength in the country. Francisco Dueñas was the last of the clerically oriented conservatives; and when he was overthrown in 1871, thanks to the intervention of the Guatemalan strong-man Justo Rufino Barrios, he was succeeded by the liberal Rafael Zaldívar. His presidency was an extremely notable one, witnessing the breaking up of the common lands, as well as the invasion by the death of his former patron, Barrios. Following Zaldívar came a series of aristocratic nineteenth-century liberals, including a Regalado and an Escalón. They more or less believed in the same ideology that guided the regime of Porfirio Díaz in Mexico: a mixture of economic liberalism and the positivism of Auguste Comte, though none of them allowed any ideology to stand in the way of governing the country for the benefit of their own social class.

One of the best of these men was Manuel Enrique Araujo, who came to power in a fraudulant election in 1911. A genuine reformer with a reputation for respecting the rights of even his political enemies, he was assassinated, for reasons never made clear, in 1913. [24]

The death of Manuel Enrique Araujo brought to power a dynasty which was to rule the country for some years, the Meléndez-Quiñónez family. The first of these, Carlos Meléndez, inherited the presidency from Araujo and then in 1915 had himself elected to the office. Ruling as a strong man, he crushed any opposition and had his brother Jorge Meléndez elected to succeed him in 1919. At the end of his term, Jorge Meléndez turned over the office of the presidency to his brother-in-law, Alfonso Quiñónez, who based his power on a rather uneasy alliance with certain elements of organized labor and the Liga Roja, a pseudo–left-wing political organization. Unable to find a suitable family member to follow him, Quiñónez turned to his lifelong friend, Pío Romero Bosque, a man whom he thought pliant enough to be easily controlled. Romero Bosque began his presidency in 1927, completing it in 1931.

21

This period after the death of Manual Enrique Araujo was notable as an age of expanding coffee markets and general prosperity, at least for the upper classes. The oligarchical regime of the Meléndez-Quiñónezes also put an end to the overthrows, the *golpes de estado*, which had been so frequent and disruptive in the previous period. Nevertheless, corruption had been allowed to flourish on a grand scale; elections were rigged, and the government existed through the power of the Guardia Nacional, the army, and the thugs of Liga Roja. Pío Romero Bosque sought to change all of this. He was no great social reformer, but he was at least an honest man who soon broke with his unsavory predecessors, going so far as to exile Dr. Quiñónez from the country. Graft was curtailed, and efforts were made toward honest government. In 1931, to cap his reforms don Pío (as he is affectionately known in this country's history) decided on holding free elections, perhaps the first free presidential election in the history of El Salvador and destined, as of the present writing, to be the last.

This election was held under the shadow of the Great Depression with left-wing, even communist, agitation growing in the countryside. The struggle was a complicated one with a number of new political parties springing into existence to take advantage of the unheard-of opportunity for free campaigning. In the end the man who won was perhaps the candidate least acceptable to the oligarchy — the wealthy, urbane, and progressive Arturo Araujo (not to be confused with the Manuel Enrique Araujo). Araujo, an engineer, had lived much abroad, especially in Britain, had an English wife and was enamored of the British Labour Party and its policies. He formed his own Labor Party for the election and talked a good deal about social reform. All of this was watched with growing nervousness by the great coffee planters and the military.

The new government took over in March 1931 and immediately ran into grave difficulties. It faced demands for back pay from civil servants and teachers, pressures from the *campesinos* for instant reform, and pressures from the oligarchy to make no concessions. More and more the regime came to rely on the stern military man who had become both vice president (first desig-

22

nate) and minister of war, Maximiliano Hernández *Martínez* (as he preferred to call himself) viewed with alarm the growing financial crisis of the government, which led to the prohibition of gold exports, and the violent clashes between the police and the opponents of Arturo Araujo that resulted in considerable bloodshed.

On 2 December 1931 a group of younger officers and their civilian supporters launched a *golpe de estado* against the regime. Araujo attempted to rally forces in the capital and then in the western part of the country, but ultimately fled to Guatemala and the protection of his close personal friend, the dictator Jorge Ubico. General Martínez was a first "captured" by the leaders of the coup, and yet a few days later he emerged as their spokesman. Just exactly how this remarkable feat was accomplished is impossible to explain to this day; but it appears that the general, known as a serious student of the occult, had more than ordinary powers of persuasion. This overthrow of the democratically inclined president occasioned widespread despair among those who sought reform.

Agitations and plans for a Marxist revolution began to grow; but before the movement could come to a head, Martínez, now the chief of state, managed to find out the underground hideout of the movement's leaders, and Martí, Luna, and Zapata were arrested on the night of 18 January 1932 in the capital. The movement was now headless, but the revolt was staged in any event, capitalizing on the unrest among the *campesinos* (many of them full-blooded Indians) in the western section of the country. Juayúa, Tacuba, Izalco, and other centers were seized by hoards of machete-wielding peasants shouting communist slogans. They looted the shops, killed a few of their more obvious opponents, but did surprisingly little damage on the whole. Rumors of torture, rape, and other atrocities spread throughout the country nonetheless. On the morning of 23 January 1931, having taken over much of the western area of the country, the revolutionaries hurled themselves at the important regional center of Sonsonate. It was an unequal contest between *campesinos* armed only with machetes for the most part and trained troops of the local garrison backed by the Guardia and other police units. The revolutionaries were totally routed, leaving many dead on the streets of the city.

The following day, General Martínez had his forces on the move, reconquering town after town, often after a bitter struggle. In all the rebels probably killed around a hundred persons, including an estimated thirty-five civilians, but the forces of order now began to take an appalling toll.[25] Soldiers of the regular army, the Guardia Nacional, the National Police, and volunteer units made up of upper-class gentlemen, relentlessly hunted down the "communists" wherever they could find them. To them, a communist was any *campesino*, especially an Indian, who could not be vouched for by some landholder as not having taken part in the revolt. Possession of a machete was often taken as a sign of guilt, even though all peasants used machetes as their everyday tool. Men were taken in big batches, tied together by their thumbs, and lined up along the roadsides or against the walls of *cuarteles* or churches. There they were machine-gunned and their bodies hauled off by ox cart to makeshift mass graves, often the drainage ditches along the roadsides. The extermination was so great that they could not be buried fast enough, and a great stench of rotting flesh permeated the air of western El Salvador. How many were killed is a matter of conjecture. After extensive research, I arrived at a figure of ten thousand, but many tell me that this figure should perhaps be doubled. Some sources even speak of thirty or forty thousand being killed. These latter figures seem inflated, but ten to twenty thousand would be a reasonable figure. This in a country whose total population was only about 1.4 million!

This frightfulness, of course, had a purpose. The planter class had long lived with the fear of a peasant revolt. So long had they systematically starved, defrauded, and brutalized the *campesinos* that they knew someday a great jacquerie would take place. Now they set out to make such an example of the failed revolutionaries that the peasants would never again think of rising against their betters. Further, the separateness of the Indian communities (such as those in Izalco) with their native *caciques*, or chiefs, and their *cofradías*, religious brotherhoods which no *ladino* could join, had always been resented. In part

24

the great *matanza* was a war of extermination against the Indian element. These events also left a permanent scar upon the people of the nation. The savage way in which the military and the wealthy have treated the peasants since that time is owing to a fear of repetition. This fear effectively stifles any thought of agrarian reform. As Alan Riding wrote in the New York Times (3 May 1978), "Whenever the peasants make the least demand, people begin talking about 1932 again."

When the killing was over, the survivors returned, very subdued,[26] to work once more on the coffee *fincas*. A great quiet settled over the country. In the presidential palace General Martínez organized economic reforms to battle the depression. He founded the Central Reserve Bank of El Salvador and the Banco Hipotecario to lend money to the farmers of the country. An organization called Mejoramiento Social was called into existence to aid the *campesinos* through a land-reform program which created Haciendas Nacionales to be parceled out among the peasantry in a manner similar to the *ejido* program in Mexico. Actually very little land was distributed, and even that was soon reconcentrated; but this land reform did serve to lessen discontent.

At the same time Martínez was a ruthless dictator whose chief aim was to maintain himself in power as long as possible through the army and the Guardia. He gained a reputation as a mysterious figure, and the nickname El Brujo (the witch doctor) by mixing up spells and potions and conducting séances in his mansion. For a long time, no serious challenge arose to the power of El Brujo. The United States, reluctant at first to recognize him, extended its blessing after Martínez went through the charade of stepping down in favor of General Andrés Ignacio Menéndez, who then held an election in March 1935 in which Martínez was the only candidate for the presidency. After that Martínez remained in office until 1944.

World War II, with its democratic idealism, its Four Freedoms, and its Atlantic Charter, created a profound impression on Central America. If the world was being "made safe for democracy" elsewhere, why not here? The result was the discontent which toppled such dictators as Ubico in Guatemala and

Martínez in El Salvador. The chief agent of Martínez's overthrow was a democratic-minded physician named Dr. Arturo Romero. When Martínez "elected" himself again to the presidency in March 1944, the *Romeristas* staged massive demonstrations of students and workers. The army revolted unsuccessfully; but this provoked a general strike, and the dictator, through his use of excessive violence, caused the situation to deteriorate further. On May 8, after a North American citizen was killed by the police, the United States ambassador advised the general to resign. El Brujo took the advice, left the country, and began to farm in Honduras. There he was killed by a workman on his estate in 1967.

A junta was then established under former President Andrés Ignacio Menéndez and Dr. Arturo Romero, who became an announced candidate for the presidency; but on October 21 Col. Osmin Aguirre y Salinas, the tough National Police chief who had helped put down the 1932 revolt, staged a coup against the junta and made himself the chief of state. In the subsequent elections of 1945, he was succeeded in a fraudulent vote by his handpicked successor, General Salvador Casteneda Castro. An attempted liberal invasion from Guatemala failed, and the general remained in control.[27]

Between the 1931 coup and the presidency of Castaneda Castro, the military had become the chief force in the politics of the country. The officers, often men from middle-class backgrounds, had found in politics the road to advancement and wealth, and had come to look upon political offices as being theirs by right of their professional training. The oligarchy, on the other hand, frightened by the events of 1932, had yielded its dominant role in politics more or less willingly to the soldiers. A tacit bargain had been struck which freed the very wealthy to look after the economic interests of the country while the soldiers ran the political show. Of course, the oligarchs did not entirely absent themselves from the government. Certain key posts, such as the Ministry of Foreign Affairs (or Chancellery, as it is called) and those ministries which dealt with technical subjects of finance and banking, were traditionally reserved for them; but those positions which controlled the armed might of the country were solidly in the hands of the officers. Under these circumstances Romero's plan to restore civilian rule upon the overthrow of El Brujo was almost certain to end in disaster.

Casteneda Castro had ambitions of being a second Hernández Martínez; but his fellow officers, seeing what was happening, removed him by a *golpe de estado* on 14 December 1948. This overthrow was accomplished by the younger officers of the army, who then proceeded to install one of their own, Major Oscar Osorio, in the presidency. This new group of officers had come to maturity during the Second World War, and many of them had been trained either in the United States or by North Americans. They fancied themselves to be professionals, technicians, and reformers; but in fact they would continue the pact with the oligarchy and protect its economic interests while making a show of social change, a system which continued almost to this day. Osorio legalized industrial unions, increased the numbers of jobs, and started a social security scheme to cover at least a small portion of Salvadorean labor.[28] Neither he nor his successors dared touch the peasant question in any meaningful way. The regime of Osorio was reformist in some other ways. It reorganized the ramshackle bureaucracy of the country with the aid of a private consulting firm from the United States and vastly improved the efficiency of public administration. Further, it encouraged the development of industry in the country and lured in several foreign firms.

Osorio and the majors had created their own political party, the Partido Revolucionario de Unificación Democrática (PRUD), which was neither revolutionary, unifying, nor democratic. This group intended to retain power in the country even though Osorio would have to step down in September 1956. They arranged to replace him in the March elections with Lieutenant Colonel José María Lemus, who had been his minister of war. Some civilian elements had planned to oppose this ticket by running Roberto Edmundo Canessa, a coffee grower who had been head of the coffee growers' association and minister of foreign affairs under Osorio; but a month before the election was to take place, Canessa's candidacy was banned and he was exiled from the country. Other opposition groups were likewise excluded, and Lemus won with very little trouble.

Once in power, Lemus proved harsh and dictatorial. The jails filled with political prisoners, as in the bad old days of Martínez. PRUD helped itself to local posts throughout the country and controlled ever seat in the national legislature. As a result a group calling itself the Partido Revolucionario Abril y Mayo (PRAM; the months refer to Martínez's overthrow) sprang into existence, made up of civilian political figures and university intellectuals. The focal point of discontent was the university; and Lemus, running true to form, could think of no better way to deal with it than to invade the university in September 1960, wounding a number of students and arresting the rector, Napoleón Rodríguez Ruiz, along with many others. Roberto Edmundo Canessa was arrested at about the same time, tortured in prison, and released, only to die shortly thereafter in the United States.

After such brutality, there was little surprise or displeasure when Lemus was turned out by a coup on 26 October 1960, fleeing into exile as a reform junta took over the country. It was 1944 all over again with civilian reformers combining with progressive military men in an effort to turn the country toward democracy. The civilians on the junta were Dr. René Fortín Magaña, Dr. Ricardo Falla Cáceres, and the later famous Dr. Fabio Castillo, all of whom were connected closely with the university.[29] They and the three military members of the governing body quickly promised free elections; and as if by magic, no less than nine political parties sprang into existence, including the organization known as PRAM which had been behind the coup, a Partido Social Demócrata led by ex-President Osorio, and a Partido Demócrata Cristiano (PDC). Only the last of these was destined to enjoy a very lengthy existence.

Unfortunately, the same reactionary forces which had been behind the coup of Osmín Aguirre y Salinas in 1945 now persuaded a clique of officers that things had gone too far. There was talk that PRAM was a "communist" organization because its leaders had been known to speak well of the new regime of Fidel Castro in Cuba. There was also a real or imaginary fear that

Osorio might make himself dictator. In any event, on 25 January 1961 the junta was overthrown in a bloody coup resisted by civilian and military elements.

Under the leadership of Colonels Aníbal Portillo and Julio Adalberto Rivera, a Directorio Cívico Militar now took over the country. They brought into being a Constituent Assembly to overhaul the old constitution of 1950; but in this assembly only the new official party, the Partido de Conciliación Nacional (PCN), had any significant participation. Nonetheless, the constitution is interesting in that it contained the trend toward state involvement in economic affairs. Under this constitution elections for the presidency were held in April 1962, with only the PCN participating. It came as no surprise then that its candidate, Julio Adalberto Rivera, became the legitimate, or at least legal, president of the country.

Colonel Rivera, despite the means he had used in coming to power, turned out to be a very able president; but he found himself confronted by grave economic and social problems, to which we must now turn in order to explain the crisis that erupted with Honduras at the close of the decade.

It did not take any particular genius to see that the country had become overly dependent upon coffee. This monoculture tied the economy of the country to a world market over which El Salvador had little or no control. As a result, from the time of General Martínez on, efforts had been made to encourage other crops. Cotton had first been experimented with in the 1920s in La Paz Department, but it aroused little enthusiasm because of high coffee prices. During the depression some successful cotton areas had come into production, but it was the arrival of DDT in the early forties that really started the cotton boom. A cotton growers' association came into existence, in imitation of the successful coffee growers' groups, to bring pressure on the government for better transportation. They were eventually rewarded during Lemus's presidency with the Littoral Road, built in 1958–60. This road across the south coastal plain facilitated the movement of machinery, labor, and cotton, causing a great increase in the acreage under cultivation. From 23,000 hectares in the 1951–55 period, the cotton land shot up to 48,000 hectares in the 1956–60 period, while coffee acreage remained almost the same.[30]

As in the earlier case of coffee, cotton expansion cut deeply into the land available for food crops. William Durham points out that throughout the history of El Salvador food crops have lost out to more profitable export crops in the competition for land. He further notes that when cotton finally declined, 57.4 percent of the land taken out of cotton production reverted to maize and other food crops.[31]

The textile firms which began to produce cotton cloth in El Salvador stimulated employment to some extent, though the work force involved remained small. Most of the money for this industry was Japanese, and the Japanese businessman or technician became a common sight on the streets of the capital city. For a while it indeed seemed that cotton would rescue El Salvador from its problems.

But as any student of the history of the southern United States could have told them, a cotton economy has built-in problems that are very difficult to solve. Cotton quickly exhausts the land unless a great investment is made in fertilizer and better farming techniques. Such investment soon proved beyond the capacity of Salvadorean growers; and as they could not pick up and move to fresh land in this tiny country, production soon began to falter. Disease added to the problem. The less technologically sophisticated and less well capitalized began to abandon cotton production. By 1966–67 half of the growers of 1963–64 had quit the growing of cotton, the number of hectares of cotton likewise fell from 100,000 to 43,000.[32]

As cotton declined, sugar replaced it as the country's second most important crop. The chief sugar region was the broad central valley from Aguilares northward toward Chalatenango. About 14,000 hectares of land were under sugar cultivation at the beginning of the sixties. In 1960 a sugar refinery was set up to process the sugar produced by the twenty-one *engenios* (sugar mills) throughout the country. Sugar prospered during the 1960s, with about 20 per cent of the total crop being exported to Honduras. Troubles with that country canceled that lucrative market, and sugar remained far below coffee as a successful cash crop.

A number of other products were grown in El Salvador: rice along the coast; henequen in the Lempa river valley; some tobacco and tropical fruits such as pineapple, and sorghum, which was sown among the corn rows for animal and human food. Cattle raising was also a perennially important part of the economy, although the cattle were generally of a poor quality. Maize remained the most important subsistence crop, with some 220,000 *manzanas* (a *manzana* is about 1.7 acres) being planted annually. As pointed out earlier, the cotton boom interfered with the production of maize, competing with it for the lowlands; but as cotton receded, maize acreage increased, although the country still imported it from abroad. In fact, despite an increase in the area devoted to production for all three of the major subsistence crops—maize, beans, and rice—the amount produced actually fell, chiefly due to inefficient cultivation and overutilization of the land.[33]

In the face of this stagnant agricultural situation, in which coffee continued to remain the dominant crop, despite all efforts to supersede it, came an enormous population explosion. The eradication of yellow fever and malaria, plus the growth of the use of antibiotics, cutting down the child mortality rate ("injections given" is a common sign in front of shops in the capital), caused the population to rise at a rate of 3.4 per cent per year. The census of 1930 listed a total of 1,443,000 souls. By 1961 this number had climbed to 2,500,000 and by the war to 3,549,000 with a projection of 8,803,000 by the year 2000. The population density of this tiny country stood at 170 persons per square kilometer, or about 400 per square mile in 1970. In the 1950s the populations of El Salvador and Honduras grew at 2 per cent a year, doubling every thirty-five years. In the more recent period they grew at about 3.5 per cent, doubling every twenty years.[34]

This was a restless, and in many cases, a desperate population with some 40 per cent being less than fifteen years of age. People were living longer, thanks to the wonders of modern science, but modern science had found no way of giving them sufficient food and shelter. Scavengers with haunted eyes poked

31

through the garbage cans in the plush suburbs of the capital. Clumps of emaciated scarecrows slept out, fair weather or foul, under the porches of downtown banks. Throughout the countryside roamed listless children with distended stomachs. Some few actually starved, but many more were kept alive to continue to suffer from hunger-induced retardation. "Death control has preceded birth control," as J. Mayone Stycos puts it.

With so many people coming onto the labor market, wages through the fifties and sixties became increasingly depressed. During the early sixties the average daily wage for a field hand was about one *colon* fifty *centavos* a day, or 62.5 cents. A woman working in the fields received C1.30, and even the salary of a *mayordomo* was only a little over a dollar a day.[35] Alastair White points out that workers on the coffee plantations of the Ivory Coast earned 20 per cent more than the coffee workers of El Salvador, despite the fact that the standard of living in the African country as a whole was much, much lower.[36] Even these figures are deceptively high; for, in fact, a *campesino* was very lucky to get a hundred and fifty days of work a year. If one estimates that an entire family worked that long they might gain a total yearly cash income of three hundred dollars by 1964.

Seeing this situation, Colonel Rivera attempted some measure of reform, in 1965 raising the minimum wage for day laborers in agriculture to C2.25. The oligarchy greatly resented this and immediately took measures to cancel its effect, forbidding the workers to farm the small plots they had previously used on the estates, dropping the traditional daily noon meal of one tortilla and a handful of beans, and laying off as many workers as possible. The situations of the *campesinos*, who were by law forbidden to organize for their own protection, was worse after the 1965 law than before.

In this desperate situation a fierce struggle over the land arose. Within 95 per cent of the nation's available territory under cultivation, this struggle focused on existing holdings. Since the expropriation of the common lands, peasants had been accustomed to defy the law and to sow their corn in any vacant area where they could, totally disregarding property rights. Even vacant lots in the cities were quickly overrun with precarious corn plantings.[37] The *paracaidistas* (parachustists), as these squatters were called, were of course resented by the great landholder and run off, even murdered, whenever possible.

One of the most famous instances of this sort of activity took place in the capital following the disastrous earthquake of 1965. A parcel of land belonging to the Dueñas family had to be leveled after the destruction of the quake, and overnight the *paracaidistas* settled in. They formed an association, calling their territory the Campamento Third of May. Its population reached an eventual seven hundred. These *campesinos* then defied the efforts of Dueñas to evict them from the land, getting a great deal of public sympathy and support, especially from the left, behind them. Baptist missionaries working in the country offered to buy the land from the oligarch, but their offer was scornfully refused. When after years of violence and litigation, the community petitioned the National Assembly in February of 1971 to legalize their position, their *campamento* was invaded and burned to the ground, thus solving that squatter problem.[38]

The *paracaidistas* simply made visible the desperate land hunger of most of the population. Officially, only 11 per cent of the land was in the hands of the peasantry, while 2 per cent of the populace owned about 60 per cent of the total land, and a mere 8 per cent of the populace got one-half the national income. While 51 per cent of all farms, a total of 107,000 landholdings, had less than a single hectare, those with 50 hectares or more occupied 60 per cent of the land, although they represented only 1.5 per cent of the existing farms. A mere 145 estates had a fifth of the nation's land, and this legal concentration was growing. One result was that the number of renters dramatically increased, 147 per cent in the years between 1950 and 1961 alone, while land ownership totals went down 18 per cent.[39]

William Durham, in his thoughtful study of the area's resources, suggests that this land concentration and the emphasis on export crops rather than food production were more important factors in the misery of the peasantry than overpopulation in any absolute sense. He found a strong correlation between child mortality and the amount of land available to the peasants in Tenancingo, which led him to conclude, "The ability of peasants . . . to survive and reproduce is strongly influenced by their access to land."[40] Only a drastic upheaval would have been able to restore the land to the small farmers in meaningful quantities; and such a redistribution would, of course, have made it impossible for El Salvador, already suffering a perennial balance-of-payments problem, to buy what she needed from the outside world. Considering that the existing population had already done great damage to the environment, it is hard to argue that overpopulation did not exist at the time of the war.

As the countryside became untenable for the growing number of the poor, the urban areas began to attract a great crush of people. In 1932 there had been around 80,000 inhabitants in the capital, which was little more than an overgrown country town. By the census of 1961, the population had soared to 280,000; and when the war of 1969 broke out, there were an estimated 350,000 persons in the capital. Alastair White points out that this internal migration was not only due to the plight of the *campesinos:* village and small-town craftsmen who had seen their wares replaced by cheap manufactured goods from the factories of the capital or from abroad also joined in the rural exodus. He further points out that women formed a disproportionately large part of this constant migration, seeking husbands in some instances, trying to get away from mates in others. Some of these female migrants were lucky enough to get jobs in the mills; but most ended up as street vendors, servants, beggars, or prostitutes.[41]

San Salvador's swelling population of indigents led to the growth of squatter communities between 1950 and 1970. Most, such as the settlement known as La Fosa, were in deep river-gullies where the land belonged to the state. Here dwellings of dubious stability were put together every which way without running water or sanitation and with only the electricity which they could illegally tap from existing power lines. By the time of the 1969 war, such shanty towns may have already held as many as twenty thousand inhabitants each. Although some of the population of such squatter settlements were newcomers to the capital, it was not unusual for people to be born there, live there during a lifetime, and die in the same hovel. White estimates that half the residents of shanty towns were born in the capital itself.[42] Also, one finding from my own investigations is that a surprising number of these shanty dwellers actually did manage to find work in the capital, earning in some cases thirty to fifty dollars a month.

In a country with such an excess of population, a North American might imagine that birth control would be vigorously pursued, but this view does not take into account the temperament of the people. Fertility is so prized that some *salvadoreños* will not eat unfertilized eggs or plant hybrid corn. A large family was the traditional source of support for one's old age and provided the progenitor of such a family with a kind of guaranteed immortality. The Church is also of course a factor in inhibiting birth control, but it is doubtful if anyone would listen to the counsels of the clergy were they not reinforcing a populatly held belief. For many years the important conservative newspaper published by Napoleón Viera Altamirano carried on an anti–birth-control campaign, declaring that "to populate America is to civilize America" and that foreigners wished to "dissect the wombs of Latin American mothers and to castrate Latin males."[43] The left comes at the issue from a somewhat different angle, declaring that without a large population they will never succeed in overwhelming the North American exploiters, and pointing out besides that land concentration is the real problem.

Limited to less than eight thousand square kilometers, and growing so rapidly in numbers, the Salvadoreans sought to escape their dilemma by immigration abroad. Over the decades Salvadorean communities built up in Guatemala and in the United States, especially on the West Coast and in New Orleans, but the favorite mecca of the immigrant was neighboring Honduras. This would lead to a decade of strife, culminating in the war of 1969 and the subsequent impasse. Before discussing why Honduras did not continue to welcome the Salvadoean migrants it is necessary to turn to the history of that fascinating land.

Chapter 3
Honduras: Land of the Midnight Coup

In theory there is a strong agreement throughout the region that the five states of Central America are but parts of a common whole. In practice there are strongly marked differences in the culture, society, and economy of each of the five. Honduras and El Salvador together, comprising approximately 51,000 square miles, would fit handily into the state of Kansas; and yet for all their seeming sameness, there are many obvious differences.

Although both are basically mestizo nations, a walk down the streets of Tegucigalpa or San Pedro Sula will soon convince the observer that the two peoples do not even really look alike. In San Salvador a six-footer can go for days without seeing anyone not obviously a tourist of his own height, but in the Honduran cities he would pass two or three people of equal stature every block. Generally these people would represent the strong nonmestizo element from the islands of the Caribbean or the North Coast, being either very blond and European looking or very dark and African.

The appearance of the country also differs from that of neighboring El Salvador. Soon after one crosses the border, the hills become steeper and the valleys deeper and more narrow. Instead of the scattered volcanic peaks of El Salvador, regular ranges of mountains become apparent, rising to over nine thousand feet in the western part of the country. These mountains, being nonvolcanic, give Honduras a much poorer soil quality than its tiny neighbor. Seen from the air, the terrain presents the aspect of a troubled sea rushing toward the viewer in broken, jagged waves of green and gray. The thought that immediately comes to mind is; How did the early explorers ever find their way into such a twisted land? But not all of Honduras bears this configuration. As one goes north, the hills diminish and finally fade away as a coastal plain appears, shading into swamp. This jungle region grows broader in the eastern part of the country, toward Nicaragua. The Honduran share of the Mosquito Coast, the province of Gracias a Dios, has almost no roads and is connected with the rest of the nation only by ship. Until the conquest of malaria and yellow fever, this North Coast, facing the Caribbean, was almost uninhabited, while today it represents the wealth of the country.

It was the lure of silver that first brought the *conquistadores* into the mountainous jungles of Honduras. Once the amount of precious metal in the hands of the native peoples had been expropriated, there was nothing to do but look for fresh deposits; and the persistence of this search paid off handsomely on 29 September 1578, when extensive silver deposits were discovered at what is now Tegucigalpa. Even today prospectors report that there are extensive deposits lying in wait for the bold and the enterprising in the mountains ringing the capital. The discovery of silver and the growth of the boom town, caused Tegucigalpa to be given the status of an *alcaldía mayor,* or provincial capital; but the whole area of what is now Honduras, along with much of eastern El Salvador, was really administered by the bishop of the neighboring city of Comayagua, some forty miles distant from Tegucigalpa. In a reorganization of Spanish rule in 1786, Honduras became an intendance, though remaining under the overlordship of the captain-general in the city of Guatemala.[1] Whoever ruled had only a precarious hold over much of the country. Indeed, the British occupied the Honduran islands in the Caribbean and parts of the North Coast through much of the colonial period, and even after independence.

Throughout the colonial period, Comayagua and Tegucigalpa had been bitter rivals, with the former generally getting the better of it; but independence from Spain settled the issue, for Comayagua chose the wrong side, remaining loyal to Spain, and thus the ascendancy passed to its rival.

Like El Salvador, Honduras had an easy time of it within the Central American Federation which emerged after the 1823 break with Mexico. While the Salvadorean José Manuel Arce remained in power, he attempted to maintain a conservative government in Tegucigalpa; but a resident of that city, Francisco Morazán, ousted his representative in 1827 and, as shown earlier, went on to lead the liberal forces for many years until his ultimate defeat and exile in 1840. On 11 January 1839 Honduras became a republic with Juan F. de Molina as its first president. He lasted until April of that year.

The short career of Molina was indicative of what was to come. Before the final break with Central American unity, there had been twenty-four separate presidencies; between 1839 and 1900 there would be sixty-four, although in some cases the same man would be president on several occasions. There were also frequent interregnums in which councils of ministers formed a ruling junta. All in all, the politics of Honduras from independence to the present moment presents a picture of despotism tempered by anarchy, and the capital well deserves its jokingly given name, Tegucigolpe.

One of the few able chief executives of the last century was Juan Lindo, who, after a brief early presidency, took over in December 1848, reformed the constitution, and managed to hang on until 1852, when he conducted an election turning over power to his legitimate successor, a very unusual event in nineteenth-century Central America.[2] Even this regime was marked by problems, however, such as the British seizing the North-Coast port of Trujillo in order to collect debts owed them by the Honduran government.

Juan Lindo had managed to anger Rafael Carrera during his presidency, and his successors enjoyed an unhappy tenancy in office until Carrera imposed his own man from his stronghold of Guatemala in February 1856, Santos Guardiola.

Guardiola, a high-handed dictator, ruled until January 1862, when he was assassinated. After his death there was the usual confusion, although the death of Carrera and the accession of the liberals in Guatemala meant that influence from that powerful quarter would be directed in a new way. The liberals in Honduras briefly gave way to the last dying surge of the old clerical conservatives when Ponciano Leiva took over late in

1873, but reasserted themselves, with Guatemalan help, when the popular Marco Aurelio Soto took over after a sanguinary civil war in 1876. As befitted his name, this president brought to the country "a real renaissance of both order and learning."[3] He lasted until June of 1880.

All this time, the landholding aristocracy had been doing well for themselves. They had realized that the basis of their power was less the control of government revenues than the control of the land itself. Soon after independence they had managed to concentrate the best land in their hands, forcing the small holder to move up into the steep and inhospitable hillsides. In the valleys the rich made the raising of cattle the economic foundation of their power, both political and social.[4] Although Honduras, as it proudly boasts, never had fourteen families, the gap between rich and poor continued to widen, with the poor being mostly subsistence farmers raising maize and beans on their little plots.

During the liberal epoch of Justo Rufino Barrios in Guatemala, Honduran presidents were forced to dance to his tune. Luis Bogran, the only Central American president to embrace Barrios' scheme of unity, lasted until November 1891, thus surviving his mentor and leading the country into a new political era, which will be discussed presently.

In the meantime, some note should be made of the incessant border problems which the country faced. Everyone knew there was an entity called Honduras, but no one knew precisely where it lay. After the breakup of Central America, its frontiers with its neighbors remained terribly imprecise, while Britain continued to claim the Bay Islands. This last issue was settled in 1859 when in a treaty with Honduras, Britain recognized these Caribbean islands as belonging to the North Coast region. The other boundary problems, particularly those with Nicaragua and El Salvador, proved more intractable.

Through the steamy jungles of the Mosquito Coast and on into the hills meander two major rivers, the more eastern of which is the Coco, or Segovia, River, while the westerly one is known as the Patuca. To this day these rivers remain the most reasonable method of egress into that impenetrable region. Historically, Honduras claimed the Coco River boundary as marking its eastern limit, while Nicaragua, seeking all the territory it could get, sought to extend itself westward to the Patuca. It might be wondered why anyone would care about such an uninhabitable region; but in fact, habitation or no, feeling ran very high, and the national honor of both sides came to be involved. Twice in the nineteeth century boundary agreements were drawn up, in 1870 and 1889; but as neither gave Honduras what she wanted, both failed of ratification in that country.

A treaty of 1894, ratified two years later, set up a boundary commission composed of both sides, plus a member of the diplomatic corps accredited to Guatemala or "any foreign or Central American public personage," and gave that commission ten years to prepare a definitive border. By 1904 part of the work had been done, but Honduras still was not satisfied with its award. At this point King Alfonso XIII of Spain was chosen as the "public personage" to work out an agreement; and on the day before the expiration of the treaty, 23 December 1906, an agreement was reached. The Coco River would be the boundary, with its east bank going to Nicaragua, including the town of Puerto Cabo at the mouth of the river. At first both sides accepted this award with fairly good grace; but a revolution in Nicaragua brought a hostile government to power in 1912, and from then on the dispute continued, with Nicaragua still claiming the Patuca line. In early 1957 Honduras decided to push her claims, establishing the department of Gracias a Dios and seizing the western bank of the Coco, including Puerto Cabo. In February shooting broke out, and there were some months of skirmishing before a cease-fire was arranged by the Organization of American States on 5 May. All this was brought before the International Court of Justice in 1960, and a judgment of 18 November upheld the original award of 1906. This was a victory for the Villeda administration in Honduras, and a setback for that of the Somoza dictatorship in Nicaragua, Somoza accepting the award with ill grace.[5]

This long dispute points out very clearly that a question of population pressures and immigration was not needed to touch off border conflict in the region. There was, at least when the conflict started, very little profit to be gained from the area by either side; but this did not deter the rival claimants from using every possible method, including force, in establishing their claims. As pointed out in chapter 1, when discussing the many Central American "civil wars," the Soccer War of 1969 has to be seen in the total climate of conflict and violence endemic to the region.

According to Dr. Jorge Fidel Durón, the venerable Honduran diplomat who is perhaps the most knowledgeable person alive on the question of the border dispute with El Salvador, the roots of the 1969 war lay far in the past. In our conversation Durón pointed to the year 1861 as being a critical one for relations between the two nations.[6] In that year, thanks to the monumental imprecision of Spanish land surveys, the neighboring *municipios* of Santiago de Jocoara (now Santa Elena) in Honduras and Niño de Dios de Arambala and Asunción de Nuestra Señora de Perquín in El Salvador found themselves in conflict over the limits of their respective *ejidos*, which lay north of the Rio Torola between what is now the department of Morazán in eastern El Salvador and that of La Paz in Honduras. "What began as a municipal problem became international," remarks Dr. Durón; and fifteen subsequent agreements failed to end it, for one side or the other always failed to ratify. It is interesting to note that Hacienda Dolores, lying in this same general region, would play a large role in the immediate origins of the 1969 war.

In 1869 a treaty was drafted on the limits of Colomoncagua in Honduras and Torola in El Salvador, encompassing much of the region mentioned above, but again it was not ratified. Similarly, in 1880 a preliminary convention was signed to delimit Jocoara and Opatoro in Honduras, and Arambala, Perquín, Polorós, and San Fernando in El Salvador. The then president of Nicaragua, General Joaquin Zavala, was named arbitrator, with Ramón Rosa representing Honduras and Salvador Gallegos representing El Salvador. It was agreed that if the *ejidos* of any of these towns were found to lie in part in the opposing country, the town would retain its lands, but under the political jurisdiction of the rightful sovereign state.[7] Like the agreement of 1869, this was stillborn.

On 10 April 1884 a mixed commission representing the two states met at San Miguel in El Salvador, signing there the Letona-Cruz Convention, as it is called from its principal negotiators, the Honduran Francisco Cruz and General Lisandro Letona. This was to establish a maritime line in the Gulf of Fonseca, where the islands had long been the subject of dispute. A Canadian engineer, A. F. Byrne, was likewise called upon to draw a boundary line through all of the disputed territory to the Guatemalan frontier. Honduras, however, failed to ratify the agreement, the legislature voting it down on 7 February 1885 because they did not like Byrne's line and accused him of being in the pay of El Salvador.

With all these discouragements and frustrations some practical result had to be reached, and in September 1886 representatives met in Tegucigalpa and signed the Zelaya-Castellanos Convention. Article 5 of this convention stated that until such time as agreement could be reached the status quo of 1884 would be respected. This, at least, was ratified and remained the basis of negotiations until 1962.

After still another failure to find the Polorós-Opatoro line in 1888, a new commission on the question of limits met at San José, Costa Rica, in January 1889, naming the president of that country as arbiter. On 11 November an agreement was made that the Salvadorean Santiago I. Barbesina and José María Bustamante would work out a border under Costa Rican supervision. They failed to agree; and a new convention, the Velasco-Bonilla, was signed on 19 January 1895 to complete their work. This convention was to run ten years, which it did, being renewed until 1916, but accomplishing, in the words of the distinguished ex-chancellor of El Salvador, Francisco José Guerrero, "no practical result." Further efforts were made at Tegucigalpa, the Peccorini-Lainez Convention was drawn up, and again a commission was formed in 1941. But the theme song always remained the same, "no practical result."[8]

Again, it is worth remembering that much of this took place before most of the Salvadorean immigrants pushed their way into Honduras, and when Honduras had fewer than a million people. The question of *los límites* may seem like a red herring to outsiders, and even to Salvadoreans, but to the Hondurans it has long been a burning issue.

While these things were going on in foreign affairs, the internal politics of Honduras was beginning to change with the establishment of two distinct political groupings. The origins of these rival parties are very obscure. William S. Stokes, in his important study, indicates that the system may have its origins in the clerical-anticlerical struggle of early independence days. The *cachurecos* (also called *calandracas* and known sometimes by their party color, blue) were the clerical party, which tended to be conservative in most things, even those not pertaining to the Church. Their enemies, who sought to secularize society, were the *coquimbos* (or reds). Both of these groups represented an oligarchy which based its wealth on cattle or mining and which provided the officers of the army as well. The liberals, like their counterparts in the rest of Latin America, may have mouthed the slogans of laissez-faire and paraded a knowledge of J. S. Mill; but at heart they were as conservative, in a modern sense, as their opponents.

When Marco Aurelio Soto took over in 1876, ending a long period of civil strife, he was the champion of nineteenth-century liberalism and resolved to formalize a coherent party structure through the club known as the Liberal League. With the blessings of Justo Rufino Barrios, Soto's successor, Luis Bográn continued this work of unification. The efforts of these men might have gone unrewarded, for organizing Honduran politicians is a little like herding mice, had not President Policarpo Bonilla established a formal constitution for the Liberal Party, which he then used to secure his triumph over Ponciano Leiva in a coup of 1893.[9]

The strong-man Manuel Bonilla, who took office in April of 1903, represented a return toward more established policies and feuded with the Liberal chief, Juan Angel Arias. José Santos Zelaya, the Nicaraguan president and a friend of the Liberal Party, then engineered Bonilla's overthrow in 1907.

The National Party was much slower to become a coherent group. While it may trace something of its origins to the old clerical conservatives, the truth appears to be that it arose as the response of the out-group which resented the Liberal Party's domination of events. President Trinidad Cabañas in the 1850s is regarded as the precursor of the Nationals; but it was Ponciano Leiva, the archenemy of Policarpo Bonilla, who first brought together the forces of opposition in any coherent way, calling his group the National Party. The party received juridical status as the Honduran National Party in February 1916, with Francisco Bertrand being the chief mover, but soon split when Tiburcio Carías Andino launched his Democratic National Party.[10]

Tiburcio Carías Andino, one of Honduras's most successful strong men, had, by the time of the 1923 elections, taken over all of the factions of the National Party and was their candidate for the presidency. Although he won a plurality of the vote, he was deprived of his victory through congressional manipulation. The customary civil war followed, and so serious did events appear that the United States decided to intervene to protect its very substantial interests. A provisional regime drafted a new constitution (the ninth), and elections were held late in 1924 which brought to power Miguel Paz Baraona, the former running mate of Carías Andino.

The regime of Miguel Paz brought a welcome breathing spell in the chaotic politics of the country, which had seen seventeen coups or attempted coups between 1920 and 1923.

Before going into the subsequent political events, which include the long dictatorship of General Tiburcio Carías Andino, it might be wise to look at some of the major economic factors which had shaped the politics of Honduras from behind the scenes.

Much of the history of Honduras is tied to the development of the banana industry, which began its tremendous expansion in the late nineteenth century. Until after the Civil War, bananas were virtually unknown in the United States. It was due to the efforts of a couple of very enterprising sea captains from Massachusetts that the fruit first made its way from the tropics. Captain Lorenzo D. Baker of Wellfleet was the first to notice the commercial potential of the curious fruit which he had put aboard almost as an afterthought in the West Indies. He convinced his fellow shipmaster, Jesse Freeman, to go into business with him in a partnership which eventually became known as the Boston Fruit Company. Under the leadership of Andrew W. Preston, a Boston merchant, the company did a thriving business in the strange but nourishing fruit; but it was only in 1899, when they bought out the interests of Minor Cooper Keith, that a really giant enterprise resulted.

Minor Cooper Keith was the nephew of the great railroad baron Henry Meiggs, who had built many of the major rail lines in South America. In 1879 his Tropical Trading and Transport Company began to ship fruit from Central America, principally from Costa Rica. The enterprise prospered, and the conjunction of this firm with the Boston Fruit Company was to produce the United Fruit Company, the greatest of all tropical fruit shippers and the hated octopus of antigringo legend.[11]

In Honduras the United Fruit Company was incorporated as the Tela Rail Road Company, founded in 1912, for the building of railways was seen by the government of Honduras as an integral part of the banana industry and as a rationale for the granting of concessions to the banana empires. In fact, of the 400,000 acres that UFCO eventually owned in the country, 175,-000 were given as a grant for railway construction, the idea being to connect the capital to the North Coast.[12] Honduras did this despite a land policy which had forbidden the alienation of national lands. The agrarian legislation of 1898 had declared expressly that Honduras retained title to national lands assigned to villages and municipalities as *ejidos*, and prohibited any alienation of land within eight kilometers of the sea coast. Further, a decree of 1902 expressly prohibited permanent alienation of land within the Tela district. But President Bertrand revoked this in 1911 and approved a large concession to the Tela Rail Road Company. Tela received 500 hectares for every kilometer of track laid. Further, the government provided such subsidies to the railways as to "almost bankrupt the Honduran state,"[13] as Charles Kepner demonstrates.

Obviously, a great deal of bribery and corruption had gone into the creation of a favorable climate for business enterprise, and one of the great corruptors was Samuel Zemurray. Zemurray was from Selma, Alabama; and while working in his uncle's

Selma store, he became fascinated with bananas—how to sell them, how to keep them, and where to get them. He moved eventually into the fruit trade in New Orleans, but not satisfied to be simply a middleman, he took a ship for Honduras in 1905. Zemurray bought land along the Cuyamel River and gained railway concessions from venal governments. When President Miguel Savila, in 1910, adopted an anti concession policy, Zemurray conspired at his overthrow, replacing him with General Manuel Bonilla, the ousted national chief.[14]

Zemurray's Cuyamel Company and the Tela Rail Road Company were certainly not the only major interests in Honduran bananas. The Vaccaro Brothers, Zemurray's New Orleans rivals, had also established themselves on the North Coast, eventually becoming Standard Fruit and Steamship Company, with its base at La Ceiba. These companies gained vast land concessions, supposedly for their railroads.[15]

In 1929 Zemurray, no longer young, decided to retire, selling out his interests to United Fruit in return for its stock; but UFCO soon found itself in deep financial trouble as "yes, we have no bananas" became the theme of the depression decade. Zemurray, to protect himself as UFCO's largest stockholder, seized control in 1932 and pulled the giant industry out of the depression. Before long United's empire was larger than ever. United's Honduran operations had covered 14,081 acres in 1918, 87,808 acres by 1924, and after the acquisition of Cuyamel, 95,300 acres. This soared to 175,000 acres during the decade of the thirties; and UFCO shipped 20,200,000 bunches out of Honduras in 1932, as compared to 5,076,920 for Standard Fruit.[16]

In their elaborate apology for the banana interests, Stacy May and Galo Plaza Lasso point out that bananas account for only 4 per cent of the total crop acreage of Honduras and that "bananas are not preempting land which might be better employed." But this is by no means the total picture. United, for instance, planted only 34,100 acres of bananas in the early fifties, but owned a total of 300,000 acres, while leasing 7,000 more. It was, by May and Plaza's own estimation, "by far" the largest enterprise in the country, contributing in the fifties over thirty-five million dollars a year to the local economy. To put it another way, in relation to the economy of Honduras, it was four times as important as was General Motors to the economy of the United States.[17] Add to this the powerful interests of Standard Fruit—and the foreign-owned New York, Honduras, and Rosario Mining Companies (the three largest enterprises in Honduras)—and one gets a clear picture of overwhelming foreign control of the nation's economy. Indeed, as Eddy Jiménez astutely points out, "Honduras has ceased to be a nation and converted itself by the grace of its governments into an American *latifundia.*" From 1925 to 1950, foreign firms took out a total of 825,-000,000 *lempiras* or L33,000,000 a year (a *lempira* being worth about fifty cents in U.S. money). In 1950 the foreign companies realized L48,600,000 from their operations, while the budget of the Honduran government was L50,000,000.[18] Whereas at one time silver had been the major export (54 per cent of the exports of 1889), by 1960 silver exports, chiefly through the Rosario Mining Company, were only 3.5 per cent of the total value, and bananas were 45 per cent.[19] The banana companies also controlled the oil, tobacco, and beer industries. With such overwhelming economic leverage, the great corporations could practically dictate to the government.[20]

The regime of the great banana enterprises was extremely paternalistic. The problems of malaria and yellow fever along the North Coast were conquered by banana-company doctors. Both UFCO and Standard paid unusually high wages of one to two dollars a day, at first to induce workers to the fever-ridden coast and then, after the conquest of disease, in order to attract the most able and efficient workers. The companies provided housing of a generally high standard, schools far better than any others in Honduras, and medical services that would have been otherwise unobtainable. This was done, not in the interests of altruism, but because it gave the companies a hold on their workers and, for a while, prevented unionization. Further, these services were not without their economic benefits. United made huge profits from its company stores, and wrote off the operation to overhead expenses, thus outwitting the tax collector.[21] It should be noted as well that through their networks of roads and railroads, of schools and hospitals and stores, the banana empires created an infrastructure for the country which would have otherwise been lacking.[22]

The large work force of the banana industry, which often rose to over thirty thousand, when Honduras had but a million and a half people, was recruited, in the early days, not so much from *campesinos* lured from the hills, as from West Indian Negroes and Caribs, coming from the Bay Islands of Honduras and other parts of the Caribbean. It was believed that these West Indians were better able to stand the climate and the diseases. As disease was conquered, the dependency on West Indian workers became less. There then grew up a tension between the West Indians and the Hondurans of mestizo stock. The reasons were partly racial and partly cultural. The West Indians, including the Bay Islanders, were English speaking, mostly Protestant, and culturally out of tune with the easygoing people come down from the hills. As a result black labor, except from the Honduran islands, was legally restricted starting in 1903, and finally prohibited altogether in 1929.[23] This led to the importation of Salvadoreans, with consequences which would be of great importance for both countries.

Altogether, the banana industry, because of its influence in government land policy, its inducements for Salvadorean labor, and its economic control of the government, would play a large part in creating the conditions which led to the war of 1969. But before discussing these points, the political history of the country should be brought up to the critical year, 1954.

Stokes, in his 1950 study of the Honduran governmental structure, commented that "the average man too frequently feels little or no responsibility for the efficient operation of government. . . . When conditions become intolerable, he reflects his discontent by transferring his loyalty from one authority to another, not by assuming responsibility himself for reform."[24] This remains true to this day, but it should be pointed out that the happy-go-lucky indifference of the masses of Honduran people is also owing to the fact that they are conscious of a political manipulation over which they can exercise no control whatsoever. The politicians, generals, and oligarchs, masquerading as Liberals and Nationals, allow almost no scope for the public voice. Elections have been a standing joke, and the secret or Australian ballot was not in use even at the time (the late 1940s) Stokes wrote.[25]

One election which was a genuine exception to the rule of force and fraud was that of 1928, which came at the end of the presidency of Miguel Paz Baraona. In that contest the Liberal Dr. Vicente Mejía Colindres ran against the National Party candidate, Tiburcio Carías Andino. The "revitalized" Liberals took the election; but for once there was no rebellion, Carías urging his followers to accept the public decision, an attitude which won him a great deal of popularity.[26]

Four years later the dynamic General Carías captured the presidency in another election in which the popular will seems to have prevailed; but unlike 1928, there was an uprising on the part of the disgruntled losers, who had to be put down by the army. Perhaps it was this experience that soured General Carías on democratic formalities; certainly, he paid scant attention to them thereafter, making himself a thoroughgoing dictator.

Imposing in physical appearance, Carías stood six-foot-four and was of heavy build. The stern-faced president was a remarkably able man. He had been the youngest participant in the Liberal uprising of 1894 and served as fiscal general of production under President Dávila (1907–11), along with being a successful farmer, a part-time military man, and a professor of mathematics.[27] He imposed a belt-tightening plan upon the debt-plagued country, launched a program of highway construction, and politically pacified the country. But having done so much, he was very reluctant to leave office, as he was constitutionally obligated to, in 1936.

Instead, he decided to use his great prestige to change the constitution, allowing the president and vice-president to remain in office until January 1943. Thus began a period of *continuismo* which, once begun, proved hard to stop. In December 1939 the life of the presidency was "continued" until January 1949, a decade away! During the sixteen years of Carías's rule, the legislature was stifled, the press muzzled, and the Liberals squelched. Nepotism and government favoritism flourished.[28]

When Carías finally decided to step down from office, his choice of a successor fell not upon his vice-president, Abraham Williams, but upon a prominent lawyer for United Fruit, Dr. Juan Manuel Gálvez, who was easily elected on the National ticket in October 1948. Gálvez was expected to be a puppet of the old dictator, but Carías retired from political life and gave the able lawyer a free hand. The new president continued the program of road building and extended the activities of the Honduran airline, Tranvías Aereas de Centro American (TACA). To aid the faltering economy, two new state banking institutions were created, the Banco Central de Honduras and the Banco Nacional de Fomento. The former was designed to generally control the economy and the currency, while the latter was a mortgage bank able to make loans to agriculturalists. To lessen the dependency on bananas, Gálvez encouraged the growing of coffee and the expansion of cattle herds. He also promoted education, badly needed in a country in which only 35 per cent of the populace were literate.[29]

But behind the facade of stability which had characterized the country since the year General Carías Andino came to power, grave economic and social problems were at work, undermining the structure of the state and producing a crisis which would last for decades. Before discussing the experience of the Salvadoreans in Honduras, it will be necessary to examine this crisis in some detail.

Chapter 4

The Crisis of Modern Honduras

At the end of the Carías era, Honduras was still a small, backward land, with a population of only 1,200,542, according to the census of 1945. Tegucigalpa was still an overgrown village of 87,000. This meant that there was theoretically plenty of land; but a great deal of it was up and down or inaccessible, and the population until 1961 was growing faster than that of El Salvador. Further, despite the claims of Honduran propagandists, the distribution of the land was as bad as that of El Salvador. The 120,266 *minifundios*, or small holdings, were equaled in size by the 436 largest of the great estates, not counting the fruit companies. To look at it another way, 8.8 per cent of landholders occupied 63.3 per cent of the total exploited land, and 0.8 per cent occupied 38 per cent. Again, as in El Salvador, there were many illegal occupations of the land. Some of the lands were illegally held by the great planters, but many were held by poor squatters. In 1952 some 17,143 squatters were occupying 133,561 hectares, or 5.3 per cent of the land. Another large segment of the rural population were the sharecroppers, and only 21.3 per cent of the 156,135 farmers in Honduras had full property rights over the land they farmed. Whatever the type of land tenure, 75 per cent of all farming units were subsistence farms, employing about 40 per cent of the population and contributing 23.3 per cent of the total agricultural production.[1]

Commenting on some of these statistics. Benjamín Villanueva stated, "These figures point up the harsh economic and political reality behind the increasing land fragmentation in traditional subsistence agriculture. They are indicative of the extent to which historical concentration of economic and political power in a few hands has produced limitations on the bargaining opportunities of the peasant class." The large, and growing, number of subsistence exploitations created a real economic, political, and social dualism.[2]

Despite the growing fragmentation of the lands of the poor, their share of the land was eroding as the share of the great landholders increased. As in El Salvador, this meant a trend away from food production toward the production of cash crops and toward cattle ranching. The number of cattle in the country doubled between 1939 and 1950 and rose 14 per cent more from 1952 to 1966, mostly on great estates. Cotton also showed a dramatic rise. To increase the land for these profitable products, the *hacendados* did not hestitate to use force and fraud. In all, as Durham's study indicates, the land-shortage problem of the small farmers was no less acute than it was across the border.[3]

In so far as Honduras had a mercantile middle class, it was dominated by the árabes, or *turcos*, as they are often called. In actuality, these people are the descendants of Lebanese Christians who fled to Central America around the turn of the century, escaping Turkish oppression. They are easily identified by such prominent family names as Andoine, Kafie, Larach, Kafati, Facusse, Bendeck, and Handal. Many of these families have branches in Guatemala and El Salvador as well, but their role in Honduras is much larger than elsewhere in Central America. A good deal of Latin "anti-Semitism" is focused on these people, who are often said to be plotting for their own economic benefit. General José Alberto Medrano, the chief of the Salvadorean National Guard during the war, told me that he believed the árabes were largely responsible for the war, and pointed out that Jorge Shafick Handal, the head of the Salvadorean Communist Party, is a member of one of the great Lebanese clans. There is actually no evidence that the árabes follow any particular political policy. Honduras also had a small professional middle class of lawyers, doctors, and professors at the one small National University.

In addition to all the groups mentioned above, a new force began to manifest itself in the 1950s, a force without parallel in El Salvador. This was the force of unionized, elite labor which would first show its strength in the great strike of 1954. Unions had been legally restricted, but they existed all the same. The

54

Federación Obrera Hondureña, founded in Tegucigalpa, had some six thousand members in 1931, while the Federación Sindical Hondureña, headquartered in San Pedro Sula, was active in trying to organize the banana workers. A railway workers' union also existed. In 1931–32 a wave of "revolutionary" strikes occurred against the great banana companies, owing to the fact that the worldwide depression had weakened the market for bananas and forced the companies to reduce salaries and work forces. These strikes played a role in bringing Tiburcio Carías Andino to power, but as far as the workers were concerned, very little was gained by them.[4]

For the most part, the banana workers continued to live in backwardness and ignorance until 1954.[5] In that year it was the influence of events in neighboring Guatemala which began to have a marked effect on Honduran labor. Guatemala, since the overthrow of Jorge Ubico, had enjoyed a decade of progressive government. Land reform policies had been instituted, and unions had been encouraged to organize. UFCO, also a major factor in Guatemala, had been forced to come to terms with the banana workers there. Not content with letting this example speak for itself, the militantly left-wing government of Jacobo Arbenz Guzmán had spread propaganda about its achievements throughout Central America and encouraged the downtrodden to rise up against their persecutors. His militancy was greatly resented throughout the region, where Arbenz and his followers were branded as "communists"; and a plan was set up, with the aid of the CIA, to overthrow the Guatemalan government. This Honduran-based overthrow would come in June 1954 after a long period of tension on the border, but by that time the propaganda from Guatemala would already have changed the course of Honduran history.

On 10 April 1954 the dock workers of the United Fruit Company struck spontaneously at Tela, demanding double time for Sunday; and by 3 May the strike had spread to UFCO operations at Puerto Cortés, La Lima, and El Progreso. The government of Gálvez declared the strikers to be "communists," as was customary, and sent troops to the North Coast, provoking violence and doing nothing to quell the strike, which now spread to

the railroad itself and to the field workers on UFCO's plantations. The banana workers wanted an increase of salary averag-
ing 50 per cent and a shortening of the work week from forty-
eight to forty-four hours. The wage of a common banana laborer
at that time was about twenty cents an hour. They wished to see
it raised to seventy-two cents an hour.

By 11 May the Standard Fruit workers had also joined in,
making a total of about 22,000 workers on strike. Nevertheless,
United Fruit decided to tough it out, declaring that there could
be no negotiations for at least thirty days and none at all while
the strike lasted. This impasse created a wave of furious resentment throughout the country, long under the tyranny of the
great corporations. The Rosario Mining Company, the Honduran
Brewery Company, and the British-American Tobacco Company,
the latter two linked financially to the fruit companies, went out
on strike along with a number of smaller firms, not only on the
North Coast but in Tegucigalpa as well. By 18 May some fifty
thousand workers were on strike. Standard Fruit then agreed to
concessions; but United, backed by the government and encouraged by United States Ambassador Whiting Willauer, continued
to make life difficult for the strikers, although it did at last agree
to negotiate.

The strikers too had their difficulties; organization was still
weak, and the leadership was divided between Manuel Valencia,
representing a more moderate wing, and Augusto Coto, a Marxist. This problem was partly solved when the government had
Coto and several of his followers arrested.

Concerned with the danger of communist subversion, the
American Federation of Labor and other international labor organizations then intervened. As the strike dragged on, both the
United States and the Honduran governments had become
alarmed that some kind of upheaval would result if no agreement were reached and so began to urge UFCO to make concessions. At last, after seventy-five days, the strike was settled, with
the banana workers gaining almost everything they had sought,
including salary boosts, paid vacations, and hospital care.[6]

The immediate results of the great strike were that bananas
worth many millions of dollars had been left to rot in the fields,

TABLE 1. UNIONS IN HONDURAS—AT END OF SIXTIES
(courtesy U.S. Embassy, Tegucigalpa)

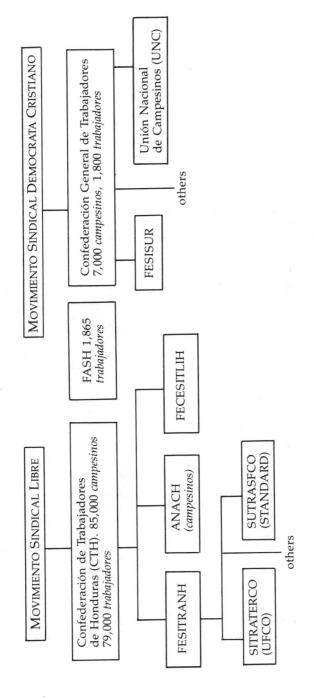

while enormous amounts were lost in wages and manufactures, but in the long run the strike greatly benefited Honduras. As William Harbin, United States labor attaché, put it, "There was no country until 1954." Out of the strike the average Honduran drew a sense of identity and pride because little men like himself had humbled the octopus of the Caribbean.

Fearing that the forces of international communism might yet triumph, the AFL-CIO took pains to help the victorious workers organize themselves into noncommunist unions. Such labor experts as Andrew McClellan were dispatched to the scene to explain how permanent organizations might be established. The attitude of the Honduran government also began to change, a new labor law of 1959 making unions mandatory in firms of over a certain size. As Leiva Vivas states, "The strike of 1954 taught profound lessons to the working class and little by little gave birth to the most powerful organization of workers in Central America."[7] Two major fruit-company unions emerged from the strike, the Sindicato de Trabajadores de Tela Railroad Company (SINTRATERCO), which is the union for United Fruit, and SITRASFCO, its counterpart with Standard Fruit. Both of these are part of the Confederación de Trabajadores de Honduras (CTH), numbering by 1978 over 160,000 workers and *campesinos*. There are also a number of other labor organizations in the country (see table 1), of varying strength and militancy.

Thus a new element was interjected into the political struggles of Honduras, an element essentially unknown in El Salvador, where labor organization has remained weak. The unions could not themselves make or unmake presidents; but along with the landed oligarchy, the army, the middle class, and the fruit companies, they became part of the power mix of the country.

They also had a good deal to say about the agrarian policies of the government. Up until the crisis of 1954, some 15 per cent of the banana workers had been Salvadoreans; but with the coming of unionization, the jobs would go to Honduran nationals. Further, as the CTH began to organize among the peasants, it demanded that a program of land reform be carried out. If, as had been the case in Guatemala, this reform were carried out by expropriating the great banana companies, the unions themselves would be the losers; an uneasy alliance, therefore, grew up which had only one safe target for expropriation: the Salvadoreans.

Any hope that political quiet could be restored after the trauma of 1954, was dashed by the events surrounding the elections scheduled for the same year. Tiburcio Carías Andino, despite advanced years, longed to return to the Disneyland-looking presidential palace in downtown Tegucigalpa. He had no trouble winning the nomination of the Nationals, but a disaffected group broke away to create the Reformista Party and run his former vice-president, Abraham Williams. The Liberals, hoping to profit from this split, put up Ramón Villeda Morales. The elections took place, with relative honesty, on 10 October, and Villeda outpolled Carías by 121,213 to 77,041. Williams ran a poor third with 53,041 votes.[8] Villeda had not, however, won a majority of the votes cast; and the election was thrown into Congress, which the Nationals then boycotted in order to prevent a decision. In the midst of this crisis, President Juan Gálvez, stricken by illness, turned over the power of the presidency to his vice-president, an aged and so far undistinguished political hack, Julio Lozano Díaz.

Owing to the failure of Congress to agree on a winner, the country seemed about to plunge into a civil war, which no one wanted. Thus there was almost relief when, on 6 December, Lozano moved decisively, declaring himself dictator. It was the same old story of someone assuming strong-man rule in order to avoid the imaginary "chaos" that would result from democratic rule. Soon Lozano even uncovered the obligatory "communist plot," allegedly backed by Guatemalan ex-president Juan José Arévalo, which allowed him to tighten the screws even more. Villeda and other Liberal leaders were exiled from the country, and an abortive coup was stifled in which over a hundred were killed.

To add insult to injury, Lozano decided to hold rigged elections for a new legislature in October 1956. With the Liberals exiled and the Carías faction of the Nationals boycotting them, the elections were an easy victory for Lozano. Nonetheless, blood ran in the streets when a group of protesting Liberals were fired on by police in Tegucigalpa. These events sealed Lozano's doom, although a compliant new Assembly elected him as legal president. On 21 October a military coup led by the younger officers unseated the seventy-one-year-old dictator, who was hustled into exile without bloodshed and without ceremony.

The men who now assumed power resembled the young Salvadorean officers who had first thrown out General Caste- neda in favor of Colonel Osorio and then gotten rid of Lemus and replaced him with Colonel Rivera. They were professionals, careerists whose whole life and devotion were to the army, as opposed to such old style part-time warriors as Carías. Their intervention was due to their belief that the army embodies the vital spirit of the nation and is, beyond constitutions and parties, the guiding genius of the *patria*. Their leaders were Air Force Commander Colonel Héctor Caraccioli, 34; Major Roberto Gálvez Barnes, 31 (the son of the ex-president); and General Roque Rodríguez, 55, the commander of the military academy.[9]

Having won power, they did not follow the precedent of their Salvadorean counterparts and try to retain it for them- selves. Instead, they began to set in motion the machinery for truly free elections to give the country a constituent assembly which in turn would choose a new president.

These elections actually took place in September 1957 and were hailed as the most honest in Honduran history.[10] The assembly which emerged was dominated by the Liberals, who promptly chose Dr. Villeda Morales as president, for six years running until 1 January, 1964. The general consensus of opinion seems to be that Villeda was a moderate and reasonable man who tried, at first at least, to improve the lot of the poor in Honduras, although the Salvadorean White Paper, with custom- ary overstatement, branded him as a man "of disloyal politics, sinuous and foreign to all moral principle."[11]

In domestic affairs he sought to curb the power of the great fruit companies and, generally, to back the unions. These policies led to periodic revolts by the right, most notably that of Colonel Armando Velásquez Cerrato in 1959. In foreign affairs the period was dominated by increasingly bad relations with Nicaragua, where the Somoza dictatorship quarreled with Villeda over the above-mentioned boundary issue and accused Honduras of aiding Nicaraguan rebels. Difficulties with El Salvador also began to increase. Through all the six years he was in office, Villeda strove to pursue a moderate course, gradually erasing his old image of being antigringo. In return President John F. Kennedy was a warm Villeda supporter, and Alliance for Progress aid flowed into the country.[12]

All this caused certain powerful forces to gnash their teeth in quiet anger. If this regime were to suceed, changes unfavorable to the oligarchy and to the fruit companies might result. Particularly vexing was the establishment of the National Agrarian Institute on 6 March 1961 and the enactment of the agrarian reform law of 29 September 1962. These seemed to threaten land 'enure changes comparable to those of Guatemala in the early fifties. Actually the National Agrarian Institute was conservative in nature and dealt chiefly with crop-related problems,[13] while the agrarian reform law was not implemented for several years. A social security scheme, Honduras's first, was likewise not really put into effective operation, but it suggested more drastic reforms to come.

Elections to pick Villeda's successor were scheduled for 13 October 1963, with the Liberal Party candidate, Modesto Rodas Alvarado, a very likely winner. If Rodas Alvarado had been elected, he would have probably continued the policies of the Villeda regime, and might have given the people of Honduras a habit of democracy. To guard against this fearsome possibility, an alliance of conservative elements was formed. It included the military, which had tasted political power in ousting Lozano and certain National Party leaders, such as Jorge Fidel Durón. Among the officers involved, the most important was the commanding officer of the air force, a dapper little colonel in his early forties, Oswaldo López Arellano. Their coup took place on 3 October, just ten days before the dreaded event, and was totally successful. Villeda was sent into exile, and López Arellano was installed as chief executive. John Kennedy refused to recognize this government; but in a short time his opinion no longer mattered, and his successor recognized the government in January 1964.

All things considered, this was the most tragic of all the long line of tragic events that make up the history of Honduras. It brought to power a man of the most sinister political morals, and led to a long period of political suppression and institutionalized violence. Out of the coup, in the rural areas came a new organization linked to the National Party, the Mancha Brava, a group of "shock troops" composed largely of public employees, "authorized to attack and kill" enemies of López Arellano's government.[14] This Mancha Brava was to maintain a shadowy existence for many years and become synonymous with government-inspired violence.

The dictator deeply distrusted the Alliance for Progress, at first refusing all aid from that source, and then after Kennedy's death, accepting it only if he could "institutionalize" it, that is, oversee the direction of it so that it went to his associates.[15] He indeed seemed to distrust everything, including his own associates. A purge was conducted after the coup which got out of office some of its chief supporters, including Jorge Fidel Durón, Adolfo León Gómez, and Luis Bográn Fortín, as well as such military men as Colonels Armando Escalón, Edmundo Pujol, Roberto Palma Gálvez, and Alonzo Flores Guerra.[16]

To regularize his position, López Arellano decided to call for still another National Constituent Assembly, to draft still another constitution and choose a president. These elections took place on 16 February 1965, and no pains were spared to make sure that the National Party would win so that López Arellano himself might be the chosen president. If the election of 1957 had been the most free in Honduran history, the election of 1965 was perhaps the most corrupt. To induce the Liberals to participate, the government invited representatives from the Organization of American States to witness the elections, an invitation which was withdrawn as soon as it had served its purpose. On the day of the elections, Mancha Brava thugs and government forces roamed the rural areas, intimidating and even attacking potential Liberal or Reformista voters. Masterminding all this was the secretary of the presidency, Ricardo

Zúñiga, an able, calculating lawyer who was the real brains behind the presidency, and a brilliant political strategist. The tactics by which the Nationals won were denounced by, among others, Bert Quint of CBS, who personally observed the elections in Danlí. In the end the party in power gave themselves thirty-five seats out of sixty-four, a figure nicely calculated to give them control, but not to drive the Liberals into open rebellion.[17]

The opposition leaders, following the election, set up a Comité Cívico Nacional, of Liberals, Popular Progressives, and the unions, but failed to block the election by the Assembly of López Arellano. The Liberals at first told their deputies to abstain in the presidential balloting, but after some political maneuvering they agreed to participate and give a semblance of legality to the ballot. Only a few, such as labor leader Céleo González, refused to cast a vote.[18]

Although the regime was now legal, if not legitimate, the president still relied on the army to maintain him in power. It is one of the ironies of the situation that it was the Liberals who first brought the professional military men into politics and who lavished funds, better spent elsewhere, to maintain a strong military machine. They were the victims, as Rafael Leiva Vivas is so fond of pointing out, of the machine they had themselves created.

While Oswaldo López Arellano might maintain himself in power with the aid of the army, the army could not control the economy for him, and forces were at work which were causing grave difficulties for the country. One of these forces was population growth: although Honduras was not overpopulated in absolute numbers, there was a definite problem of age distribution. The natural increase was just over 3 per cent, but with the Salvadorean immigrants this was raised to about 3.3 per cent by the middle of the decade. The result was that with a life expectancy of only fifty years, every other person was under fifteen and had to be supported. Poverty, as pointed out above, remained very great, with the average *campesino*, discounting those unionized workers of the great fruit companies, earning on an average about $200 a year, giving the median family a total income of $250 a year. This increasing population was being squeezed more and more by the increase of cattle raising and cotton production.[19]

The discontent of the peasantry was being manifested in the seizure of government and fruit-company lands along the North Coast. In some cases these seizures were violent, and in many cases the subsequent expulsions were by force. *Campesino* discontent was as potentially explosive in Honduras as in El Salvador, and UFCO began to pressure the government to find some solution to the problem.[20]

To complicate matters still further, the large landholders banded together to form an anti*campesino*, antisquatter, and above all anti-Salvadorean group in 1966. This was the Federación Nacional de Agricultores y Ganaderos de Honduras, which is generally shortened to the sinister-sounding word FENAGH. This group was and is dedicated to the preservation of the great landholdings, and to their furtherance through the seizure of lands. As the Salvadoreans were often squatting on public land and were fair game, FENAGH launched a great propaganda campaign against all things Salvadorean. The history of Honduras in the late sixties is one of a see-saw battle between FENAGH and the agricultural unions, such as ANACH and UNC, which sought to win back the ancient *ejidos*.[21]

A second major problem for López Arellano was the growing balance-of-payments deficit. This was in part due to the Central American Common Market. As César A. Batres, who has played a leading role in the revival of the economy, explained it to me, the Common Market caused Honduras to turn from the United States as a supplier of many imports to Guatemala and El Salvador, although these countries sold products of lesser quality and higher price. The reduced tariffs made this possible; for although the base prices might be higher, when import duties were added to the prices of United States goods, it was the latter which were more expensive. If Honduras had been able to offer comparable products in return, there would have been no problem; but the products of Honduras were either such things as fruits and minerals, which went to the United States, or cattle and cotton, which duplicated the products of El Salvador. The one other product which might well have been sold to El Salvador, maize, was itself in short supply in Honduras. In 1967 Honduras had to *import* twenty thousand tons of maize from Mexico.[22] Thus the balance of payments problem grew.

From table 3 it can be seen that despite Honduras' blaming all its woes upon the MCCA, it ran almost as large a trade deficit with the United States (Canadian trade is minimal) as it did with Central America. Thus in actuality Honduras remained as much as ever an economic colony of the United States; but it could not easily attack the source of its arms, its loans, and its banana revenues. El Salvador offered a more convenient target. Nonetheless, the problem in regard to Central America, and in particular El Salvador, was very real. In fact, by 1969 the economies of the five countries had become so imbalanced that only Guatemala and El Salvador enjoyed favorable trade balances in Central America, while Costa Rica, Honduras, and Nicaragua presented negative trade balances.[23] In 1965 the five countries had launched a study for restructuring the half-decade-old Common Market; but it came to nothing and, according to César Batres, forced Honduras into an untenable position.

As Stycos pointed out, "There began to emerge among intellectuals the uneasy feeling that Honduras was becoming El Salvador's colony in the traditional economic sense,"[24] or as one prominent Honduran scholar of the National University remarked to me, "We didn't have dollar imperialism, but *colón* imperialism." This was not strictly true. In fact, as table 4 below indicates, the figures put out in 1972 by the MCCA show Honduras exporting more to El Salvador than it received until 1966. But it was perceived as true not only by university intellectuals but also by the man on the street. It was accentuated by the fact that while North Americans remained relatively remote figures, Salvadoreans were visible everywhere, in large numbers, competing for jobs and for land. If the trade balance had been the only reason for Honduran feelings of animosity, they could have equally been directed against Guatemala, with which it had a trade deficit of L11,300,000, or L1,100,000 more than its deficit with El Salvador.[25]

It is perfectly possible that if all trade had not been shut off between the two countries, the imbalance might have reversed

TABLE 2
BALANCE OF TRADE OF HONDURAS [26]

1963	1964	1965	1966	1967	1968
-L23,585,000	-L15,671,000	-L9,345,200	-L7,133,400	-L13,389,400	-L4,001,300

(the *lempira* being worth 50¢ in U.S. money)

The breakdown of these figures in regional terms for 1967 gives an even more revealing picture.

TABLE 3
THE VALUE OF EXPORTS, REEXPORTS, IMPORTS, AND THE BALANCE OF TRADE FOR HONDURAS WITH SELECTED AREAS 1967 (in *lempiras*) [27]

Area	Exports	Reexports	Imports	Balance
Central America	446,794,871.51	2,101,379.18	481,507,527.16	-32,611,276.47
North America	139,677,975.26	1,542,385.81	163,817,037.68	-32,596,676.61
Europe	102,028,511.86	17,950.12	53,954,015.76	+48,092,446.22

TABLE 4
VALUE OF TRADE OF HONDURAS/EL SALVADOR (In millions of
Central American pesos)[28]

	El Salvador to Honduras	Honduras to El Salvador
1959	4,299	6,470
1960	4,124	6,299
1961	4,644	6,577
1962	5,734	10,414
1963	7,851	10,772
1964	8,956	13,016
1965	12,264	15,682
1966	16,335	13,343
1967	19,872	12,369
1968	23,236	14,838
1969	12,415	7,339

itself in time. In fact, the Common Market provided very real benefits to Honduras even in the short run. Jeffery B. Nugent's work on the MCCA hypothesizes that an annual growth rate of 1.8 per cent in El Salvador and 1.3 per cent in Honduras was attributable to participation in the Common Market. The MCCA not only increased trade within its boundaries but also stimulated trade with the outside world and led to a modest diversification of products.[29] Certainly, the countries had become more interdependent and less dependent on the United States. In 1953 El Salvador imported 59.9 per cent of its imported goods from the United States, and Honduras an incredible 71.6 per cent, while importing only 9 per cent and 3.7 per cent respectively from Central America. In 1968 El Salvador imported 31.4 per cent of its goods from Central America, and Honduras 26.3 per cent, while importing only 29.4 per cent and 45.9 per cent respectively from the United States. Exports to the United States had made up over 70 per cent of the foreign trade of both in 1953, but only 19.6 per cent for El Salvador and 43.9 per cent for Honduras in 1968.[30] All the same, Honduras viewed the Common Market as a great evil.

It is impossible to say definitely what the economic situa-

TABLE 5

INCREASE IN GNP WITH/WITHOUT ECONOMIC INTEGRATION[31]
(Figures for 1962–68, prices constant)

	With integration (real)	Without (hypothetical)
El Salvador	5.8%	4.6%
Honduras	6.6%	6.0%
Central America	6.5%	4.9%

tion might have been in El Salvador and Honduras without the Common Market, but the MCCA itself published some interesting figures in 1972 to suggest that the Market was good for both countries from the standpoint of their gross national products.

A third major economic problem was the national debt, which was growing to truly catastrophic proportions. It stood at L51,330,426 at the end of 1966, and L1,846,302 was being paid in interest. The economy still continued to sag; and instead of curbing borrowing, the government of López Arellano took out extensive loans, including L3,143,000 from US-AID to build access roads in the agricultural zones and L3,627,000 from the Inter-American Development Bank to maintain roads. These loans pumped fresh money into the economy, created jobs, and made things look better than they were.[32]

Still another problem was the lack of public investment. Actual public investment in 1966 hovered around $10,000,000, while the projections of government economists thought that it ought to be about $35,000,000. As a percentage of the GNP, it fell from 3.4 per cent in 1963 to 2.4 per cent in 1966.[33] The impact of this lack of public investment fell mostly upon the poorest classes of the populace. Forty percent of school children were without schools, and only 1.8 hospital beds existed for every thousand persons.[34]

On 24 May, 1967 the head of the Superior Economic Planning Council, Miguel Angel Rivera, made a report which rocked the nation, outlining the lack of public investment and blaming it on lack of interest by the government, nepotism, and lack of planning.[35] This aroused the anger of the powerful secretary of the presidency, Ricardo Zúñiga, never a great fan of Rivera, whom he considered a brash upstart. Under Zúñiga's influence

López Arellano refused to listen to these justifiable criticisms, and Miguel Angel Rivera resigned in July.

All this increased public discontent and worsened the crisis. The unions and the opposition parties became more active. A series of incidents at Las Guanchías, where the Asociación Nacional de Campesinos de Honduras (ANACH) was trying to prevent the take-over of peasant holdings by the Compañia Agrícola Sula, solidified this opposition. SITRATERCO leader Oscar Gale Varela and Céleo González of FESITRANH denounced the bullying of their fellow unionists in speeches on 2 September. The government attacked all this as communist agitation and responded with arrests and repression.[36]

Municipal elections were scheduled for 31 March 1968, giving some hope of a return to democratic procedures; but it was not to be, for López Arellano had no intention of giving any power to the out groups. Again gunmen were very much in evidence, although Martín Pérez, the honest president of the elector tribunal, appealed unsuccessfully to the chief of the armed forces, Colonel Andrés Ramírez Ortega, to stop the violence. However, in the northern zone Colonel Juan Alberto Mélgar Castro made a name for himself by trying to curb the excesses of the Nationalists. In the end the Liberals gained only 35 out of 260 mayorships; and there were widespread demands, by such people as Oscar Gale Varela, that the elections be annulled. The government, confident of its military backing, disregarded all protests.

Some voices, such as that of César Batres, president of the National Association of Industries and himself a National Party member, called for the opening of a dialogue with the Liberals; but it was not to be. A few attempted meetings convinced the president that there was nothing to be gained, and the attempt was dropped. In a further high-handed move, the government imposed a new tax on consumers.

The upshot was a general strike on the volatile North Coast, led by the CTH. This soon spread to merchants, urban workers, and students, not only in San Pedro Sula but in the capital as well, where the university became a center of opposition to the regime. Such a strike is often, as in the case of the overthrow of Hernández Martínez in El Salvador and Ubico in Guatemala, the prelude to a coup; and the government responded on that assumption, declaring a state of seige and arresting Céleo González, the president of FESITRANH, and putting Gale Varela under surveillance. The repression was brutal, with the armed forces even invading the sacred precincts of the university and attacking the professors.[37] In the end the strike failed; and Céleo González was exiled from the country, though as a conciliatory measure the government agreed to lower the taxes, especially the consumption tax, which had a good deal to do with sparking the uprising.

Although this particular storm was weathered, the government still tottered, and the country was on the verge of chaos. In the late spring of 1969, a new wave of strikes, which lasted until the war, broke out. These focused upon the school teachers, a downtrodden and unhappy lot, and their students, who were also organized in an association. All this adds some point to the Salvadorean contention that López Arellano used the war as a means of turning attention from the internal crises of the country. The Hondurans, of course, make the same claim in regard to the government of El Salvador. But while the problems of El Salvador were basically much graver than those of Honduras, discontent before the war was not so open, thanks both to the vigilance of the Guardia and to memories of the 1932 bloodbath. It appears doubtful that López Arellano actually wanted a war to extricate him from his errors and his brutalities, but he certainly fastened on the Salvadoreans living in Honduras and on the economic benefits of the MCCA to El Salvador as a means of turning attention from his own mismanagement. It is to this story that we now turn.

Chapter 5
Immigration and Reaction

Long before population was a problem in terms of absolute numbers, Salvadoreans were leaving their country for Honduras. This was due to the extinction of the *ejidos* and the concentration of land and wealth in the hands of the few. To leave was easy enough; the *campesino* family could fit their goods in a sack, and the only tool the man needed was his machete. As for the border, not only was it undefined but also unguarded; and there were many trails, along which a small party, on foot, could slip from one country to the next. Once in Honduras, although they could have probably passed themselves off as natives, the immigrants generally did not do so. They were proud of their Salvadorean birth and saw no reason to hide in a country that welcomed them.

The basic lure was the North Coast. Starting around 1895, desperate for labor, the banana companies offered attractive wages, in Central American terms, to foreigners, not only from El Salvador but also from the islands.[1] When the government took steps, after the turn of the century, to stem the flow of West Indians, the pace of Salvadorean immigration to this region quickened. As old-timers like to recall, this move was always referred to simply as "going to the North Coast," never as "going to Honduras." So anxious was Honduras to have the traditionally hard-working Salvadoreans that in 1906 the government offered free land, unencumbered by taxes, to immigrants who would farm in remote parts of the country.[2]

In addition to the attractions of the North Coast, there were jobs to be had in the mines of central Honduras, not too far from the border. The Butler Mining Company, the Rosario Mining Company, and other enterprises brought in a steady stream of immigrants until after 1918. Among those who made the trip to the mining camps was the father of Fidel Sánchez Hernández, the man who would be president of El Salvador during the 1969 war. ⌐Sánchez Hernández likes to recall this fact about his *campesino* father and says that he himself always felt considerable affection for Honduras⌐

There was more to the encouragement of Salvadorean immigration than simply a need for willing workers. Dr. Policarpo Bonilla, president of Honduras in the late nineties, was "a noted Centralamericanist" who dreamed of fostering the integration of the region through the exchange of labor.[3] Despite the frequent border clashes among the Central American neighbors, a great deal of this kind of idealism remained long after the time of Policarpo Bonilla.

The conquest of malaria and yellow fever on the north coast and the coming of the United Fruit Company caused a major surge in migration after 1912. But as the numbers of immigrants swelled, their lot often declined. An article in the San Salvador newspaper *Patria* on 2 August, 1929, complained that "the problem of the *campesinos* and workers who emigrate to Honduras is chaotic. . . . the masses endure the worst kind of existence." On the other hand, the same paper boasted a month earlier of the inroads that Salvadoreans were making in Honduran commerce. "Our artisans, especially, are highly regarded for their fine work and industriousness and almost all the small industries on the coast belong to them. In machine and carpentry shops the Hondurans employ many Salvadoreans, even giving them preference." Everett A. Wilson estimates that at this time Progreso, Tela, and other towns along the North Coast had a population that was half Salvadorean.[4]

As the numbers grew, the attitude of the Honduran government began to shift. H. Roberto Herrera Cáceres points out that while Honduras tolerated this immigration, as a sovereign nation, it sought to limit it. Thus, the Salvadorean consul-general in Tegucigalpa reported that the government of Honduras was demanding proof of nationality from all Central Americans entering the country.[5] This was at a time when the population of El Salvador was no more than 1,400,000 and that of Honduras much less.

Several contradictory myths have grown up around this vast migration. One view is that the Salvadoreans who came to Honduras were mostly skilled craftsmen, artisans, and shrewd merchants who, through sheer hustle, edged out even the crafty Lebanese and gained control of a disproportionate share of the wealth of the country. For this reason the Salvadorean merchants were viewed with even greater suspicion than was attached to the *turcos,* and such Salvadorean firms as the shoe company ADOC were bitterly resented as part of an economic penetration. Carías claims that the small businesses in the cities were taken over by the immigrants and that they controlled 60 per cent of the grain transporting and selling, a vital item indeed in Honduras.[6] While there were some successful Salvadorean merchants and businessmen in Honduras, it seems highly unlikely that they controlled anything like the resources that were popularly imagined. But this belief made it easy for the government of López Arellano to focus hatred against all those who had come from the neighboring land.

The other side of the coin is the equally popular belief that Salvadoreans who emigrated were mostly dirt-poor Indian peasants fleeing from their cruel landlords and the savage repression of 1932. In this view the majority of the peasants went not to the North Coast, but became squatters on government lands, which covered three-fourths of the territory of Honduras. Once in illegal possession of these lands, they farmed precariously until driven off by the *terratenientes* who bought the land from the government.[7] There is certainly something to this. A great many Salvadoreans did squat on national land, just as David Browning points out they did in their own country. Many did go to the North Coast, and until 1954 they were active there in the banana fields. On the other hand, by no means the majority of those who emigrated found work in the banana regions either. The typical Salvadorean immigrant remains an elusive figure; but it seems unlikely that the average newcomer was absolutely destitute, for in that case it would have been impossible to travel. On the other hand, it does not seem likely that it was the prosperous peasant farmer or small shopkeeper who moved to Honduras. More likely, the new arrivals probably represented that ambitious but impoverished middle group of *campesinos* who sought to better their position by change.

Sometimes it was the advent of a new crop which drew them. After 1950 the cotton crop was greatly expanded in Honduras, as it was in El Salvador. Landholders went so far as to ask the Salvadorean consul to send labor because the Salvadoreans were more experienced in the work and had greater abilities, according to the consul's own recollections. It might also be noted that many of the cotton fields were owned by Salvadorean companies, which naturally preferred their fellow countrymen as workers.[8]

Jiménez, quoting a Salvadorean study on this immigration, claims that 95 per cent of all immigrants into Honduras came for economic reasons, and of the total arriving 51.5 per cent were unemployed at the time they left El Salvador. 45.5 per cent sought to better their economic status; and in fact 85.5 per cent of all imigrants had, in their own judgment, bettered themselves.[9] Stycos, interviewing refugees at the time of the war, recorded such reasons for emigrating from El Salvador as, "We were under the domination of the rich. We couldn't afford the rent they were asking for land. . . . It used to be that the rich would rent you land and take part of the crop in return. Now they only rent to the cotton growers, not to the poor." Some 75 per cent of these same people declared that they had worked "their own land" in Honduras.[10]

During the presidencies of Carías and Gálvez, there was very little trouble about this immigration. But with the seizure of power by Lozano, a strong animosity toward the Salvadoreans began. In his period a law was passed which stated that no foreigner might buy land less than forty kilometers from the coast or the frontier, an effort to keep foreigners out of the banana regions and also to guard against the gradual alienation of lands along the undemarcated frontiers.[11]

It was under the presidency of the Liberal Dr. Ramón Villeda Morales that the situation deteriorated still further, which explains the strong antipathy toward Villeda that one still notes in El Salvador. With the internal population of Honduras growing at an alarming rate, a loss of jobs in the banana industry, and an unfavorable trade balance, thanks in part to the MCCA, Hondurans began to feel the pinch of competition from abroad. Don Jacinto Pohl h., formerly the Salvadorean consul in Honduras, declared that assaults then began not only by vigilante groups but also by the Guardia Civil Departamental and the Guardia Civil Móvil. In November of 1959, almost an entire decade before the war, there was an exodus of some three hundred Salvadorean families, escaping the harassment of Hondurans. The overthrow of Villeda's constitutional government by the army in 1963 actually caused a temporary improvement in the situation, as López Arellano took firm steps to end the physical violence. But Salvadoreans had by this time become a convenient target for Nationals as well as Liberals, and while the violence abated, the propaganda against them was stepped up.[12]

It should be remembered that El Salvador was not the only focus for the growing xenophobia of Honduras. The fifties had witnessed severe border tension, first with Guatemala, before the overthrow of Arbenz, and then with Nicaragua, during the Villeda era. It was the encouraging popular response to these incidents that caused the politicos to see the usefulness of an antiforeign stance.

Francisco José Guerrero, who worked for the Salvadorean foreign ministry during the sixties and became foreign minister himself at the time of the war, says that he believes that the idea of a massive expulsion of Salvadoreans dates at least to 1962. In that year the foreign minister of El Salvador went to Honduras with several of his staff to discuss the immigration question with President Villeda. This led to the Treaty of Immigration of Amatillo, 24 July 1962. By this the government of Honduras agreed to allow those Salvadoreans in the country to go unmolested; but it was, says Dr. Guerrero, a dead letter as soon as it was signed.

After the seizure of power by López Arellano, efforts to improve the lot of Salvadoreans were renewed on a large scale, and appeared at first to be very promising. The temporary end of the attacks on Salvadoreans seemed to indicate the good faith of the new chief of state. This resulted in the Declaration of Marcala, 24 July 1965.

This declaration came about as a result of a personal meeting between Presidents Oswaldo López Arellano and Julio Rivera, at Quinta Florida near the Honduran border city of Marcala. They met there in an atmosphere of considerable cordiality and made the following statement:

1. The two presidents declare it indispensable for progress and normal development in both countries to strengthen more firmly the relations which exist between the peoples and governments. . . .
2. They declare themselves actively behind the realization of the Central American Common Market. . . .
3. They express their intent to work to intensify rapprochement and mutual cooperation. . . .
4. The presidents of Honduras and El Salvador agree to energetically oppose communist infiltration. . . .
5. The presidents of both brother republics agree to increase the efforts of their governments toward the permanent regulation of the question of immigration. . . .
6. The presidents of Honduras and El Salvador declare that these conversations took place in an atmosphere of exceptional comprehension and good will.
7. . . . The presidents of Honduras and El Salvador fraternally salute the presidents of Guatemala, Nicaragua, Costa Rica and Panama.

The Reunion of San Miguel (El Salvador) ratified this and declared that no persons would be expelled solely for lacking documents giving them legal residence.[13] Following Marcala, work on the immigration treaty proceeded rapidly, and it was signed on 21 December 1965. Article 1 declared, "The nationals of either of the two contracting parties, which today subscribe to this treaty, who find themselves installed in the territory of the other party may not be the object of expulsion for lack of documents which legally accredit their residence." It added, however, that persons lacking legal papers when the treaty would take effect should obtain them. Further, nationals of either contracting party entering the country of the other after the date of the treaty had to obtain proper entry papers from the consulate in the host country. Both parties agreed to prevent illegal immigration.[14] Salvador ratified promptly, but Honduras hesitated more than a year before finally having its legislature ratify the document on 25 January 1967.

At this time two other important negotiations were going on. One concerned the revision of the Common Market agreements, as previously mentioned; the other concerned the still undefined border with El Salvador.

Now that the Nicaraguan border at last appeared to have been stabilized, Honduras turned its attention to its southern boundary. In that area of rugged hills, deep ravines, and swift streams, even Mason and Dixon would have had trouble drawing a satisfactory line; but in 1962 the two countries involved decided to have a go at it. A mixed commission on frontiers was established, including such luminaries as Jorge Fidel Durón of Honduras, probably the most knowledgeable person on this issue, and René Padilla Velasco of El Salvador. The mixed commission was given the task of preparing a draft agreement on how to go about fixing the boundary line over this verdant and rugged terrain. The commission began its work on 5 September 1963 and continued working until June of 1967. In December of that year, a draft treaty was passed from the Hondurans to the Salvadoreans; and *La Prensa* (27 February 1968) quoted Padilla Velasco, the secretary-general of the Salvadorean boundary commission, as declaring that "notable advances" had been made and a treaty was soon to be expected. There, however, the matter dropped. El Salvador never returned the document, and the war subsequently intervened. The two sides, at the end of 1978, had still not agreed on how to go about the business of actually drawing a line; still less of course have they been able to make any actual boundary surveys.

What ultimately wrecked all the good diplomatic work done by the conscientious chancelleries on both sides of the border, was the decision of Honduras to apply the agrarian reform law of 29 September 1962 in a manner hostile to the interests of the Salvadoreans living in Honduras. But before that decision was made in 1969, a number of things had occurred which led toward the ultimate breakdown of relations. Back in 1961, on 6 March, the government of Villeda had created the National Agrarian Institute. This body, as pointed out earlier, was not intended to effect radical economic transformations. The setting up of this body was followed by the agrarian reform law, which stated in Article 68 the following:

> The *campesinos* who meet the following requirements are eligible to receive a parcel of land by donation:
> 1. Be Honduran by birth, male over sixteen years if a bachelor or any age if married, or a spinster or widow if caring for a family.
> 2. Have as his habitual occupation agricultural work.
> 3. Not possess in his own name and in freehold land equal in extension to or greater than the total donation.
> 4. Not possess an individual capital in industry or commerce greater than L1000.00 or an agricultural capital of more than L2000.00.

The key point of Article 68 is contained in Section 1 which limited those eligible for government donations to persons born in that country. When the government got around to applying the law in the late sixties, this article was used not simply to give land to Hondurans but also to evict Salvadoreans who had squatted on government land. Shortly after this law was passed, however, Villeda was overthrown; and the government of López Arellano, which was conservative and not really propeasant, tended to sit on the legislation.

Further, the Pact of Amatillo offered an interim solution to the problem of Salvadorean immigrants by regulating immigration, opening a number of new consular offices to ratify immigrants, and by declaring a three-year grace period for Salvadoreans to legalize their status in Honduras.

But the issue of the immigrants had by now captured the public imagination, and although it had first been used by the Liberals, politicians of every hue soon took up the outcry. The leader of this anti-Salvadorean feeling was Modesto Rodas Alvarado, who launched a public campaign against the influence of Salvadoreans in the country. By this he meant not only the immigration but also the economic penetration through Salvadorean businesses and through the unfavorable trade balance produced by the Common Market. Although many persons from El Salvador remained secure in possession of their lives and property, many others began to feel the effects of this hostility. The newspapers began to speak of a Salvadorean fifth column within the country.[15] The Mancha Brava reared its head again, to such extent that on 5 June 1967 *El Pueblo* (Tegucigalpa) complained of its anti-Salvadorean activities and spoke of the "Social disintegration" which would result. Although some Hondurans, such as the knowledgeable Virgilio Gálvez, insist that the Mancha Brava was *"un fantasma,"* it seems clear from the frequent references to it that it did signify a terrorist tendency among those allied to the government, although it may not have ever been an organization in any formal sense. It was especially strong in Olancho where Colonel Lisandro Padilla, a powerful political figure, was the ringleader of the antiforeign movement. Some immigrants were physically attacked; many more were threatened in the years between 1963 and 1967.

One mischievous element in these attacks was the landholders' group, the Federación Nacional de Agricultores y Ganaderos de Honduras (FENAGH). As previously mentioned, FENAGH, founded in 1966, was designed to resist peasant demands for land reform and to continue the process of extending the great estates, by means fair or foul. The Salvadoreans, as Durham notes, were the most vulnerable section of the peasantry; and it was relatively easy for FENAGH, behind the mask of patriotism, to turn *campesino* discontent against the Salvadoreans. This, as Carías and others have pointed out, led to a curious inversion in the roles of the oligarchies in the two countries toward their respective peasant elements. The Honduran oligarchy could persuade its *campesinos* to attack Salvadoreans, thus ultimately provoking a war, while the Salvadorean *catorce* could get the peasantry there distracted from a program of land reform by drumming up a national war with Honduras. In the most polished version of this scenario, the two oligarchies enter into a kind of tacit conspiracy for this purpose. But FENAGH was by no means the only culprit in this story.

For in the meantime other pressures were building up for the enforcement of the agrarian reform law. These came from the Asociación Nacional de Campesinos Hondureños, FESITRAN, the Confederación de Trabajadores de Honduras, and the Ligas Agrarias of both the South and the East: all powerful parts of the unionized labor force and voices which even an antilabor government could not afford to ignore, especially one in as deep economic trouble as that of López Arellano.[16]

On 24 December 1966 ANACH called upon the government to enforce the dormant agrarian reform law through the Instituto

Nacional Agrario, a cry which was taken up by other segments of union labor.[17] This was at a time when the ratification of the new immigration treaty was hanging fire. When that was ratified in January, the intensity of the chorus increased. "Now we will have more Salvadoreans than Hondurans," thundered the headlines in *El Pueblo* on 16 February. The anti-Salvadorean feeling appeared especially strong in Yoro and Olancho provinces, where large amounts of acreage had been set aside to take care of the proposed paper mill's needs. Many Salvadoreans had entrenched themselves on these lands and were thus felt to be holding up the progress of the country.

In 1967 a much more serious problem developed. For years there had been intermittent struggle along the frontier, as this ill-defined area was the natural haunt of bad men of both countries who preyed upon the nationals of the neighboring territory with relative impunity, drifting back across the border to avoid arrest. Cattle stealing had become a fine art in the region, and was often attended by bloodshed, pillage, and rape. The Salvadoreans, having much more highly organized paramilitary forces, had tried to dominate the border with Guardias Nacionales, frequently ignoring the de facto border and crossing in hot pursuit of supposed felons. Not only the police but armed civilian vigilantes sometimes found their way across. These *guanacos* (as the Hondurans contemptuously call their neighbors) had invaded the departments of Ocotepeque, Lempira, Intibucá, and La Paz, seizing lands and holding them by force. Mercedes de Oriente, in La Paz beyond the Rio Torola, was said to be especially hard hit.[18]

As the clamor to expel Salvadoreans from lands in Honduras grew, so did alarm over border crossings. *El Pueblo* announced on 17 February 1967, the day after it had complained so strongly about immigrants, that a force of Guardia had crossed the Torola. This border penetration was turned back; but it emphasized the interrelation of the border problem and the immigration problem, for to Honduras both were symbols of Salvadorean aggression.

In those days a ranch known as Hacienda Dolores lay between the Rio Venado and the Rio Lajitas, which merge to form the Torola. This ranch was either in the Honduran province of La Paz or in the Salvadorean province of La Unión, depending on whose version of the frontier one wished to believe. The proprietor, Colonel Antonio Martínez Argueta ("colonels" breed in Honduras faster than in Kentucky), at least believed he was Honduran, and paid his taxes in La Paz. [19] In that locale he raised cattle, along with his brother Ricardo and his brother Mariano (known as "the old fox"). Their herds were often augmented by strays from across the border, and when those failed, they had been known to indulge in a little casual rustling. What else they might have done was a matter of conjecture; but if one can believe *El Diario de Hoy* (San Salvador), they were "like something out of the films of Pancho Villa" (18 July 1967), making savage cruelty a way of life. The paper accuses them of torturing their victims, "always cutting off their noble parts," of raping women, and of destroying property in El Salvador. All this, of course, is denied by prominent Hondurans, who came to see in Antonio Martínez Argueta a victim of Salvadorean treachery. One thing is certainly true: the border was the haunt of many criminals of both nationalities, and many vicious crimes were committed on Salvadoreans and Hondurans alike. The various leaders of these outlaw gangs lived in many ways like the border lords of medieval Scotland, always managing to slip back into their own country to evade the law.

On 25 May 1967 a party of Salvadorean National Guard, supplemented by local vigilantes, came up the north bank of the Rio Lajitas, under the direction of Colonel Eduardo Casanova and José Vicente Bonilla, the *alcalde* of Polorós. In the early hours of the morning, they fell upon Hacienda Dolores, and there arrested the fifty-five-year-old Antonio Martínez Argueta, along with his uncle and *mayordomo*, Antonio Argueta Romero, plus Fermín López Martínez and José Elías Rodríguez, who were workers on the cattle ranch. Martínez Argueta was charged with the 10 July 1961 murder of Alberto Chávez, the *alguacil* (town marshal) of the neighboring Salvadorean village of Lajitas. He had been indicted for this crime in absentia.

It need hardly be said that there are two different versions of the death of Alberto Chávez. According to the Salvadorean *juicio penal*, [20] the *alguacil* was shot "various times" at Cantón Lejitas while performing his police duties against Martínez Argueta. The Honduran version is that Chávez was shot

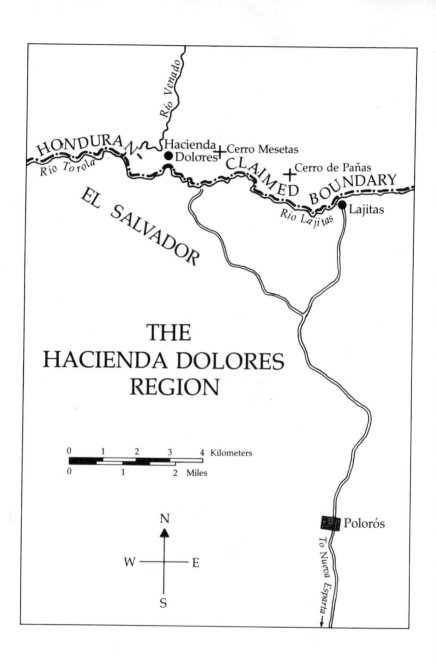

THE
HACIENDA DOLORES
REGION

down by members of the local constabulary while committing "acts of depredation" in Honduran territory.[21] Certainly, there appeared to be plenty of evidence at the time that Martínez Argueta was involved in the death. In any event he was taken from Hacienda Dolores to Nueva Esparta and turned over to judicial authorities, following which he was tried before a criminal court and sentenced on 11 July 1967 to twenty years in prison.

This was no ordinary case, and Colonel Martínez Argueta was no ordinary man. He was not only rich but a close personal friend of the president of Honduras, Colonel Oswaldo López Arellano, who was a fellow native of La Paz. Their relationship was so close that at the time of the incident, the Salvadorean press declared they were actually relatives; but this appears not to have been the case, though they were *compadres*. To make matters still worse, it was quite apparent that the Salvadorean patrol had violated Honduran territory in order to lay hands upon the border bandit. In this regard the Honduran argument is unassailable: if Hacienda Dolores were in El Salvador, why did the Guardia have to wait six years and then sneak up on the ranch as if invading foreign territory? Clearly, the decision to arrest Martínez Argueta was made on the highest levels and was a deliberate response to the violations of Salvadorean rights in Honduras.

There were other provocations in the same period. The very day that the alleged murderer was arrested there was a violent clash at Florida which is said to have left four Salvadorean Guardia and an equal number of Honduran defenders dead. Four days later, the Guardia made a second raid on Hacienda Dolores and burned it to the ground.[22] All this led to heated exchanges between Tiburcio Carías Castillo, the Honduran chancellor (foreign minister), and his opposite number, Alfredo Martínez Moreno.

But worse was yet to come. In the early hours of 5 June 1967, far over on the western frontier where both El Salvador and Honduras meet Guatemala, four army trucks rumbled into the border village of El Poy, and then right on through across the border into Ocotepeque, Honduras. Incredible as it might seem, there appear to have been no border guards on either side of the frontier, which is clearly marked not only by signs but also by a bridge across the Quebrada de Pacaya, and by a marked change in the quality of the road. The force which made the crossing consisted of two officers, 1st Lt. Eric Mauricio Sosa Portillo and 2d Lt. Inocente Orlando Montaño. With them were thirty-nine enlisted men and four civilian drivers.[23] This entire convoy continued eight kilometers to the provincial capital of Nueva Ocotepeque and parked in the town square between the *alcaldía* (town hall) and the parish church. There, according to contemporary accounts, they meekly surrendered to the municipal commandant upon being informed that they were in Honduran territory. The claim of the two officers involved, which they later restated at the official investigation, was that they had both been asleep in the trucks, and did not realize that they had crossed the border. This explanation of the whole incident was so preposterous on the face of it that the two were later nicknamed in the popular press as *Las Bellas Durmientas* (the Sleeping Beauties), a term coined by Ricardo Dueñas in *El Diario de Hoy.* Despite their outrageous admissions, neither was dismissed from the service, both continuing to serve in the army until Lieutenant Montaña was killed in a parachuting accident and Lieutenant Sosa was found shot under mysterious circumstances. Whatever they knew about their real mission, they carried it with them to the grave.

To put the situation in proper perspective, it is necessary to remember that Fidel Sánchez Hernández had just been elected as the successor to Julio Rivera in El Salvador. He was to take office on 1 July, the traditional inauguration date. His election over Abraham Rodríguez had been filled with bitter controversy, charges of fraud, and accusations of dictatorial military rule on the part of the PCN. Between the election and the first of July had occurred the Martínez Argueta incident, which deeply embittered relations between the two countries. At the same time in Tegucigalpa, López Arellano was the subject of bitter criticism by the Liberal opposition and the unions. Putting all this together, several possibilities emerge.

One idea which has been suggested is that the Nueva Ocotepeque incident was manufactured by dissident members of the military, irked at the selection by Rivera of Sánchez Hernández and hoping to prevent the inauguration of the latter. It is hard to imagine who might have gained from this within the military of El Salvador, when every effort was being made to present a united front against the leftist opposition. However, the Honduran ambassador, Virgilio Gálvez Madrid, in a cyphered telegram to Deputy Foreign Minister Carlos H. Reyes noted that "it has been suggested in various circles in this country (El Salvador) that both actions (Dolores and Ocotepeque) were maneuvers of politicians and military men to prevent the inauguration of Col. Fidel Sánchez Hernández."[24]

Another, more paranoid, version appears in a book by José René Barón Ferrufino, who claims that the Ocotepeque incident was an attempt of the Communists, in league with Presidents Rivera and Sánchez Hernández to stir up trouble in Central America for their own benefit.[25] Juan Ramón Ardón's book likewise sees the invasion as the work of the two Salvadorean leaders, either as a "pretext for armed aggression" or as an ill-conceived attempt to supply arms for a Salvadorean fifth column within Honduras.[26]

An explanation which seems more likely is the one supplied to me by a high-ranking official of the Salvadorean foreign ministry who was himself closely concerned with these events.[27] It seems that López Arellano was very put out by the arrest of his friend Martínez Argueta and decided on a plan to grab some hostages of his own. The scheme was truly Machiavellian: The important Honduran garrison town of Santa Rosa de Copán was the headquarters of the commandant of the third military district, Col. Arnoldo Alvarado Dubón. On 22 May 1967 there had been an incident of violence in Tegucigalpa, when his son Oscar Armando Alvarado had apparently shot an officer, but was himself killed by Capt. Moisés Reyes Arellano, a close associate of the president who was acquitted subsequently.[28] This made it seem plausible that Colonel Alvarado might lead a coup against the unstable government of López Arellano. Thus the government of Honduras hatched a plot in which Colonel Alvarado was to send word to the military in El Salvador of such intentions, in an effort to lure some soldiers into their hands. He told the Salvadoreans that a number of garrisons would rise up, but that a certain amount of military aid would be necessary from El Salvador. Vexed with the migration problem, Rivera and Sánchez Hernández (the president-elect and real leader at this time) took the bait. They arranged with Alvarado to supply troops in the Ocotepeque region and elsewhere along the border for a projected coup on 5 June. Thus the elements which crossed the border at El Poy were part of a much larger plot. This is somewhat substantiated by an urgent cyphered dispatch which Ambassador Gálvez sent to the Chancellery in Tegucigalpa at 2:00 A.M. on the morning of the fifth. "I have information that today two battalions have been sent toward the frontier . . . with campaign equipment. Possible destination San Miguel." The Salvadorean White Paper also admits that troops had been put on general mobilization the night *before* the incident occurred, "to preserve the sovereignty of the menaced fatherland."[29]

Some points, however, remain obscure. A document in the Honduran Chancellery files, dated 19 April 1968, speaks of "a large quantity of military implements: bazookas, machineguns, submachineguns, carbines and munitions" being captured with the Sleeping Beauties. The inventory from the secret files of José Antonio Pérez, the chief of security, lists two 9mm machine guns, four 51mm mortars, fifteen Madsen light machine guns, and twenty-one Mauser rifles, plus a great deal of other military hardware. This may have meant that the troops were planning to equip anti–López Arellano civilians, or it could simply have been their own personal store of weapons. The meek arrest of the troops is also a problem. The aforementioned official of the foreign ministry of El Salvador stated that the troops were not arrested in Nueva Ocotepeque at all, but simply picked up the local commandant as a guide and then drove on to the *cuartel* of Santa Rosa and there were disarmed by the entire garrison. This would seem the most likely story, but is contradicted by a document which was found by myself and an associate at the *cuartel* of Nueva Ocotepeque in July 1969 which actually describes how a handful of Honduran soldiers disarmed and arrested the intruders, being forced to hit one of the lieutenants over the head with a gun butt. Father Roderick Brennan, the missionary priest who was the pastor of Nueva Ocotepeque, and whom I interviewed there during the war, said that he witnessed the arrest in Nueva Ocotepeque. So embarrassing was this easy surrender that the Salvadorean press fantasized "170 soldiers hidden on roofs around the central plaza" (*Prensa Gráfica*, 15 June 1967), but the truth apparently is that once the soldiers realized they had been tricked into Honduran territory, they accepted the idea that the game was up and turned over their arms with but token resistance.

The capture of the Sleeping Beauties intensified the tensions between the two countries. There were now more than forty Salvadoreans languishing in the barracks of Santa Rosa (evidently in rather cushy circumstances) while Martínez Argueta and his companions rotted in the Salvadorean prison. Attempts were made to downplay the importance of all this, with General José Alberto Medrano, the chief of the Guardia, declaring in *Prensa Gráfica* (27 June 1967) that "it appears to be a mere police incident on the frontier, explicable in a zone where no definite demarcation exists. In my judgment it is a diplomatic, not a military problem." This was not at all what he believed, but it served to quiet the war fever which grew daily more intense. Jittery Ambassador Gálvez had sent a confidential coded note to his government on the twenty-first, stating, "I have to inform you of intense military activity in different zones of this country. It is necessary to put our armed forces on the alert."

Medrano's statement appears to have set diplomatic wheels in motion. Chancellor Alfredo Martínez Moreno declared in *Prensa Gráfica* on 17 July that "the matter is being investigated with a true sense of historical responsibility and conscientiousness within the canons of the law." The minister of defense, General Fidel Torres, stated that "the government of El Salvador is undertaking a coordinated action by all its means to reach a definitive solution to the frontier question" (*El Diario de Hoy*, 18 July 1967). The signal from El Salvador was definitely that some accommodation could be reached. Even the Church got into the act, with Monsignor Luis Chávez, the aged archbishop of San

Salvador, and his counterpart in Tegucigalpa, Héctor Enrique Santos, petitioning for a meeting between Sánchez Hernández and López Arellano (*Diario Latino,* San Salvador, 29 June, 1967).

The situation remained grave despite these various feelers, and the activities of the Mancha Brava continued apace. When El Salvador protested against this violence against its nationals, Tiburcio Carías Castillo (the Honduran chancellor who had replaced Roberto E. Quiros, and the son of the ex-president) launched a counter accusation to Martínez Moreno, complaining that El Salvador was "violently and unjustly" expelling Hondurans in the province of Chalatenango.[30] Within El Salvador there began to be asked a good many questions over the government's handling of the whole issue, with the PDC deputies in the legislature especially making trouble. In the March 1968 municipal and legislative elections, the PDC carried a great many localities, substantially increasing its representation in the legislature and on the municipal level.[31] It was increasingly obvious that the government would have to move effectively to release its captured troops.

In that same March, Dr. Francisco José Guerrero, a distinguished lawyer, became the foreign minister of El Salvador, and began to move toward an accommodation. But it was difficult to overcome the hostility and suspicion on both sides. On 1 June his Honduran counterpart, in an interview with *El Cronista* (Tegucigalpa), declared that Martínez Argueta was the innocent victim of public furor and "anti-Honduranism which, disgracefully, exists in many elements of the neighboring country although disguised by words, words, words of loving Central American fraternity." He accused the government of El Salavador of disrespect for the government of Honduras and hatred for the Honduran people.

Nonetheless, quiet diplomacy was at work on all the outstanding issues. The Salvadorean ambassador to Mexico, Héctor Escobar Serrano, presented to President Díaz Ordaz the idea that he might act as the arbitrator of the boundary problem, an idea with which Honduras concurred.[32] A fortunate occasion now arose for bringing together the principals in the dispute over the captives. The Organization of Central American States (ODECA) had scheduled a meeting in San Salvador for early July, and President

Lyndon B. Johnson of the United States was to attend as a gesture of goodwill, and in hope of resolving the Honduras–El Salvador dispute. Quietly, through the good offices of the United States, a deal was worked out, with a decree of amnesty for Martínez Argueta being presented to the Salvadorean legislature by its president, Francisco Peña Trejo. The PDC representatives and other nongovernment members bitterly opposed this move, but the ruling PCN had enough votes to pass it. Before the assembled delegates to the meeting of ODECA, the Salvadorean minister of justice declared, "The events which have occurred are a grave menace to peace between the two countries and a serious cause for deterioration of the progress made toward Central American integration and in such circumstances it is the duty of the government to seek means for pacific solutions to re-establish harmony between the two countries."[33] Moved by this gracious speech, López Arellano, who was present along with the other leaders of Central America, declared that he would free the Sleeping Beauties. President Johnson, in attendance along with Lady Bird and Lucy, was deeply pleased by the turn of events, as were, no doubt, North American business interests in both countries.

Martínez Argueta flew to Tegucigalpa on 6 July, arriving, by coincidence it is said, at the same time as López Arellano. The airport was crowded, "the family of Antonio Martínez Argueta having waited since the early hours of the morning." All in the crowd were "visibly moved by the return of their compatriot," who was embraced by his president and fellow native of La Paz (*El Cronista*, 6 July 1968). Two days later, the prisoners of Nueva Ocotepeque, along with two Guardia and three *campesinos*, were delivered to El Salvador.[34] The hapless lieutenants had to face a court of inquiry, but the general feeling on both sides of the border was that a crisis had been passed and things would now take a turn for the better. In reality there was worse, much worse, to come.

89

Chapter 6
Land Reform and Expulsion

With the fall of Miguel Angel Rivera, the most important figure in the economic councils of the Honduran government came to be the engineer Rigoberto Sandoval Corea, who became director of the Instituto Nacional Agrario in 1968 with the blessings of Ricardo Zúñiga. Sandoval remains to this day a controversial figure, hated of course in El Salvador, but widely admired in his own country, not only for his accomplishments in the field of land reform but also for the enemies he made. Ferrufino, who seems to find communists under every bed, declares that he was "a known communist with various years of residency in many socialist countries, including Russia and Czechoslovakia"[1]; but while it is true that he had been much abroad, such charges appear absurd. J. Mayone Stycos, in his thoughtful book, points out that he benefited some 17,000 families in the first two years he held office, putting 2,300 on fully organized cooperatives. During his period some *campesinos* increased their yearly income from $230 to $1,185. Further, when the *hacendados* broke into his communes, he sent them packing, despite threats and intimidation, including the murder by wealthy landholders of his right-hand man in September 1970. His showpiece was the commune of San Bernardo in southern Honduras, designed as an "ideal *hacienda*" with workers' cooperatives and shared equipment.[2] In 1971 Sandoval was to be dismissed by López Arellano's successor, probably because he had succeeded all too well.

The instrument for Sandoval's activities was the agrarian reform law cited in the preceding chapter, which at the end of 1968, after so long a period in limbo, began to be applied in earnest. But the method of application, given the conservative nature of the López Arellano regime, would have to take into account the power of the great landholders and the banana

91

companies. As Francisco José Guerrero remarked to me, "Engineer Sandoval found it easier to take land from the Salvadoreans than from the landlords."

Indeed he did; and as a preliminary to expelling the Salvadoreans, many of whom were squatters, he sent around officials of the INA, who declared to the Salvadoreans that they wished to help them "regularize the titles" to their land, and asked how many years they had been in Honduras, what documents they had, the size of their family, the numbers of their cattle and other beasts, even how much they had in the bank.[3] The unfortunates who could not come up with proof of prior title soon received the following message:

> We are sad to say that, upon making a study of the condition of present inhabitants of these lands, you are among those persons who may not be beneficiaries of our Law of Agrarian Reform, since the law establishes, as the prime requisite *being Honduran by birth.* Nonetheless we welcome this opportunity for you to demonstrate to us your real condition to be such, but in the case that this is not so, this study shows that you have illegal possession of lands, moreover that they are precisely in that zone where the execution of an important agrarian project is planned for development.

The letter goes on, in similarly polite language, to give the victim thirty days to leave the land.[4]

In April 1969 the director of the INA declared publicly that the institute would proceed immediately to order Salvadorean *campesinos* dispossessed of their lands, although many had cultivated them for many years. Sandoval declared that he was applying Article 68 of the agrarian reform law, which did indeed state that only born Hondurans might lay claim to national lands. El Salvador, becoming aware of the intentions of the INA and feeling that they constituted a grave menace to the thousands of *campesinos* and laborers from El Salvador, sent engineer Jaime Chacón, director of the Institute of Rural Colonization in El Salvador, to Tegucigalpa. According to the Salvadorean report, the Honduran government assured Chacón that its land reform measures were not directed against Salvadoreans and the government of El Salvador need not be concerned with the problem. Nonetheless, by the first of June some five hundred families had been officially dispossessed.[5]

Not only were the lands forcibly taken from the squatters, but in many cases the rest of their possessions were also taken. Knowing what was coming, their neighbors refused to buy their cattle, chickens, or equipment, expecting to get all of it for nothing when they were expelled. In some cases a measure of brutality was used to effect the expulsions, and government thugs, the so-called Mancha Brava, participated in these acts of violence.

The Honduran press, moreover, now began to whip up sentiment in favor of the INA and against the Salvadoreans. *Diario Tribuna Gráfica* announced that there had been an extraordinary session of the press group of Tegucigalpa in which the editor-in-chief of that paper had proposed a resolution asking the honorable assembly and its members to go on record in favor of the National Agrarian Institute in view of its energetic decision to confiscate the Honduran lands which Salvadoreans had taken illegally. The resolution, of course, passed. *El Cronista*, on the same date, headlined, SALVADOREANS CLEANSED FROM TEN TOWNS IN YORO. The paper went on to declare that "the National Agrarian Institute, in application of Art. 68 of the Law of Agrarian Reform, as announced on May 2 of the present year, will continue an effective cleansing of the alarming number of Salvadorean *campesinos* who have infiltrated our soil as direct instruments of the fourteen little kings who leave the people of our neighboring country of El Salvador abandoned and fleeced."

The paper noted the ten towns in Yoro from which Salvadoreans had been purged as being La Mina, Agua Blanca Sur, La Sarrosa, El Bálsamo, Arena Blanca, El Jabón, La Siete, El Socorro, Quatro de Marzo, and La Seis. It also declared that there were nine other towns in the provinces of Santa Bárbara and Copán from which the Salvadoreans would be expelled, "as they have been from Monjarás, Buena Vista, Ola, La Llanitos, Cedeño and Punta Ratón in the Department of Choluteca." The same paper, on 18 June, declared that eighteen *aldeas* in Yoro had been cleansed of *guanacos* (a somewhat derogatory term for Salvadoreans).

Not only did the daily papers chronicle the expulsions with an unseemly glee, but broadsides began to appear in the streets of the cities and towns of Honduras. One very typical one read as follows:

　GUANACO: If you believe yourself decent, then have the decency to get out of Honduras.

If you are, as the majority are: a thief, a drunkard, a lecher, crook or ruffian, don't stay in Honduras. Get out or expect punishment. In Honduras we don't want *Guanacos* and, if, because of your complaints to the OAS, the government must accept *Guanacos*, the people ought to reject them.

It should be noted that the press in Central American countries is a much more effective instrument of propaganda than it is in the United States. In Central America television sets are few, and most of the news absorbed by the man on the street comes through his daily paper. Further, with so much of the population ill educated, the written word takes on a kind of sacred character: if something is in the newspapers it *must* be true. Therefore, it is hardly surprising that a hysterical wave of anti-Salvadorean sentiment swept through the country.

What remains unclear is the role of the government in all this. Honduras was certainly a dictatorship, with the press functioning under the sufferance of López Arellano, and it would be hard to imagine that this campaign did not have his blessings. Faced by repeated strikes, most recently that of teachers and university students which lasted until the war, and a continuing economic crisis, it seems likely that the clever general sought to turn the wrath of the people away from himself and onto the Salvadoreans.

During the period of the Salvadorean expulsion, on 15 May, Governor Nelson Rockefeller arrived in Tegucigalpa as part of his tour through Latin America for President Nixon. The idea of sending any man, no matter how honest or able, with the last name Rockefeller was appalling. Trouble should have been expected, and trouble was what he got in Tegucigalpa. As he conferred with López Arellano in the gingerbread castle, a hostile mob of anti-American, pro-Cuban students gathered. Soldiers blocked their way to the presidential palace and, as the crowd surged forward, shot and killed one young demonstrator. Later, a crowd of a thousand burned a North American flag and staged a march on Rockefeller's hotel. In the minds of many Hondurans, as a broadside commented, the United States was "humiliating the people of Honduras" through the OAS and the MCCA, stealing Honduran money and forcing the Salvadoreans upon them. López Arellano and U.S. Ambassador Joseph J. Jova, were very glad to see the last of Rockefeller. Because of tighter security in El Salvador, his visit there had been almost unmarred.

In the midst of all this came the games which were to give the war its name and to confuse the outside world into believing temporarily that the conflict was some kind of comic-opera battle over soccer. The World Cup eliminations were going on that spring and summer, and Honduras was slated to play El Salvador in a best-of-three-game series. The first match took place in Tegucigalpa in the bowllike stadium that sits at the base of the hill surmounted by the classical Peace Monument. The Salvadorean team arrived the night before and lodged in the Hotel Prado. There they were "serenaded" all night by a hostile crowd blowing whistles, shouting, and shooting off fireworks. It was not the most sporting attitude in the annals of the game, but it was harmless. Honduras won the match. The second game was played at Flor Blanca stadium in San Salvador on 15 June. The Hondurans lodged in the Gran Hotel, and for two nights a really frantic crowd kept them, and all the rest of us living in the neighborhood, awake with a similar serenade. El Salvador, it need hardly be said, won that game handily.

It is a testimony to the tremendous popularity of *fútbol* in those countries that a great many Hondurans actually came across the border to see the second game, filling the hotels and guest houses of the capital. Sensing the mood of the crowd, many of these stayed right in their lodging and watched the game on television. For those foolish enough to go to Flor Blanca, there was a good deal of trouble. Most of this trouble was not all that serious. In his defense of the Salvadoreans, Joseph E. Maleady, the president of the United States Residents' Association, wrote in a pamphlet that "the Honduran spectators were submitted to 'the Brooklyn raspberries' [*sic*]. Apparently, some stones were thrown."[6] Actually, things were a bit more serious than that. Many Salvadoreans had thoughtfully provided themselves with water bombs made with urine and other equally ingenious devices to be used whenever they thought they could identify a Honduran. Two persons were seriously hurt. These were Elías Molina Meza and Dr. Gustavo Cruz Torres, both Hondurans, with Molina Meza receiving a broken nose and Dr. Cruz being injured badly enough to be hospitalized. Some vehicles were also damaged.

The Honduran press, of course, made the most of it, showing endless pictures of Molina Meza's bloody nose. Radio Tegucigalpa spoke of "the enormous quantity of vehicles destroyed, of violated women and sadistic beatings, of men brutally wounded by the crowds" being reported by those returning from the games. The government, it declared, "asks of the people the greatest serenity in the face of the crisis which confronts the country." *El Cronista*, as usual, outdid everyone else, speaking on 19 June of hungry and thirsty Hondurans being served urine and manure, of women stripped and violated in the streets by Salvadorean mobs. Those of us who were there saw nothing of the kind, but it was impossible to intrude any rational statements into the Honduran press.

Tiburcio Carías Castillo, the Honduran chancellor, fired off a strong note of protest to Francisco Guerrero, his Salvadorean counterpart, speaking of grave events which put in jeopardy the mental and physical well-being of the National Football Team of Honduras.[7] He also wired Galo Plaza Lasso, the OAS secretary-general, in a similar vein, declaring that Honduras formally denounced the actions of the Salvadorean mob.[8]

All this brought down upon El Salvador an investigation by a Subcommittee on Human Rights of the Organization of American States, made up of Professor Manuel Bianchi, Dr. Justino Jiménez de Aréchaga, Dr. Luis Reque, and Dr. Guillermo S. Cabrera. Ironically, El Salvador had been calling for the subcommittee to visit Honduras for some time in regard to the expulsions, but it was only after the second soccer game that the group made its appearance, with El Salvador to be visited first and Honduras second. It is not unlikely that the influence of the North American banana companies played some part in the decision. The subcommittee arrived in San Salvador on 4 July and stayed only until the eighth, going on to Tegucigalpa. As far as Salvadorean conduct during the second game was concerned, the group concluded that "during the second game in San Salvador there took place brutal aggressions against Hondurans who were attending the same, which led to serious crimes and profound offenses against the Honduran national anthem and its flag." They added: "We cannot affirm that these censurable acts were provoked or urged by the national authorities of El Salvador, but such authorities revealed a notable passivity in the face of these aggressions."[9]

Because of the tension, it was decided to move the deciding soccer match out of Central America and to play it at Aztec Stadium in Mexico City. There, if anyone still cared, El Salvador defeated Honduras on Sunday, 29 June.

Meantime, in Honduras the response to the Salvadorean actions of the thirteenth to fifteenth of June was, in the words of the Subcommittee on Human Rights, "a wave of aggression and violence against Salvadorean residents in the said country (Honduras), their properties and industries, leading to brutal excesses and the commission of grave crimes, provoking a literal exodus of Salvadoreans in the country . . . under the most painful circumstances."[10]

This was all too true. The Honduran newspaper *El Pueblo* on 18 June declared that groups of individuals had dedicated themselves to sacking Salvadorean stores, saying it was an act of reprisal for the barbarous acts committed by the Salvadorean crowds on the occasion of the football game celebrated in Flor Blanca Stadium. It added that many honorable persons had been attacked by irresponsible groups. *El Día*, another Honduran paper, ran pictures on 17 June showing the looting of an ADOC shoe store. On the nineteenth *El Pueblo* editorialized:

> An irresponsible speaker has said that the independence of Honduras began on 16 June 1969 and not on 15 September 1821, afterward the same person distorted the truth and dared to affirm that those who assault private property are the true patriots of this nation. . . .
>
> The condemnable deeds of which our fellow nationals have been victim (during the second game) are not attributable to the entire

Salvadorean people and still less to those citizens who have made Honduras their true homeland. We know of citizens of that country who have lived with us for ten or twenty years, married to Hondurans and with Honduran children who have been practically tossed out in the street by rascals who are motivated not by patriotic ideas but by a hidden desire for pillage.[11]

Still other conciliatory voices were raised. On 27 June the Honduran Ministry of Foreign Relations released to the press a statement by its ex-ambassador to El Salvador, Dr. Manuel Umaña Paloma, a leader of the Liberal Party, who declared himself to be profoundly moved by the merciless treatment given by the Honduran government to his dear Salvadorean brethren. But this was probably not the way the average Honduran felt during this period of crisis.

As we are about to enter into the recounting of certain atrocious events, it would be wise to put things into perspective by stating that the level and intensity of these crimes have often been exaggerated. On the Salvadorean side of the border, I myself and many others knew Hondurans who lived peacefully in El Salvador throughout the crisis. To give an example, in a recent conversation Rosanna Zambrano (now a researcher at Spanish University, but then a Honduran schoolgirl in El Salvador) recounted that her family had not the slightest trouble and actually crossed the border on a safe-conduct the day the war started. Similarly, Hondurans whom I know and trust assure me that many Salvadoreans went through the war in that country without molestation; and of course perhaps a hundred thousand Salvadoreans continue to live in Honduras to this day.

Nevertheless, the accounts cited from *El Pueblo* are amply documented from other sources. On 2 July 1969, upon his return after the break in diplomatic relations, the Salvadorean ambassador recounted to his chief that he personally witnessed the first persecutions, about the eighteenth, when Salvadorean vendors were set upon in the markets of Tegucigalpa. In many cases the security forces urged on the crowd. Although he saw no murders, he claims to have heard of many rural killings which took place between the fifteenth and twenty-third of June, especially in Catacamas (a major city of Olancho) by the commandant of the fifth military zone, Colonel Lisandro Padilla. He notes that on 15 June communication with the interior was suspended until the nineteenth, perhaps so that word of the killings would not leak out. He tried to persuade the diplomatic corps in Tegucigalpa to intervene in a meeting held at the residence of the Spanish ambassador and presided over by the papal nuncio. He further stated that the United States ambassador, Joseph Jova, went to see López Arellano concerning those Salvadoreans who had been detained and that the president agreed to release them, though this was not in fact done. Monsignor Héctor Santos, according to Mélgar Pinto, also intervened to ask that the Salvadoreans be treated with humanity.[12]

The Salvadorean ambassador himself protested to Carías Castillo on 20 June in a letter in which he spoke of violations, hangings, castrations, lynchings, and other crimes, and urged López Arellano to change the situation.[13] How serious these charges were is hard to say, but there are no less than forty-three bound testimonies, notarized with witnesses in Nicaragua, to which some of the Salvadoreans had fled; and these documents speak eloquently that at least isolated instances of barbaric terrorism took place.

One case is that of Eduardo Dordely Rodríguez of Chinchanote, department of San Marcos de Colón, who claimed to have returned home to find a red smear painted on his house; entering, he found his sons, aged one and two years, hanged, and his wife dying with her breasts cut off. This was attested to before *licenciado* José Manuel Domíngez, in Nicaragua on 30 June 1969. Similar testimony was taken from Miguel Angel Orellana Cardoza, forty-year-old Salvadorean farmer residing at Santa Rosa de Copán. He declared to the notary that he saw five compatriots killed, some boys tortured by having their testicles squeezed, and that he knew of women having their breasts cut off and of others violated. He stated that some were mutilated by having their nostrils slit.

A declaration taken in El Salvador at Nueva San Salvador on 1 July 1969 from Francisco Murga Galdámez of Catacamas, Olancho, declares that he was captured on 26 June and accused of being a guerrilla; but he and others escaped from the *cuartel*, although two of their number were killed in the attempt. He then headed for the Salvadorean border; but at Jutiquile, Olancho, he stopped with Señora Berta de Morales, evidently a Salvadorean. There he saw five members of the Departamento de Investigaciones Nacionales (DIN–the Honduran secret police) arrive in a Land Rover. He hid himself and watched as the DIN men approached Señora Morales and asked her whether she was a *guanaca* or a *catracha* (that is, a Honduran). Being foolish enough to answer that she was a Salvadorean, she and her two daughters, Marta and Alicia, were stripped and violated. Murga Galdámez, seeing what was happening, ran to inform her husband, Señor Alfredo Morales Mojica, who was some four blocks away. He came running with his machete, but was shot and wounded and then assaulted. Murga Galdámez then fled.[14]

In addition to the notarized documents, Salvadorean government files contain the reports of the vice-consuls in various areas. A letter from Francisco Dheming, the consul in Santa Rosa de Copán, to Chancellor Guerrero on 30 June 1969, outlined what happened to him. On the twenty-ninth he was called upon by the commandant of the third military district, Lt. Col. Arnoldo Alvarado Dubón, who brought with him two Honduran reporters. Alvarado Dubón questioned Dheming about what he had seen, and the consul told the reporters that the colonel had in fact given orders not to persecute Salvadoreans. He cited an instance on 16 June, the day after the second soccer game, when a crowd set out to lynch him, but Dheming managed to escape to the *cuartel*, where he was protected by the commandant and a platoon of police chased the mob away. Safely over the border, Dheming commented to Guerrero, "The occurrences in Santa Rosa de Copán show with total clarity that the Honduran authorities, if they had wanted, could have avoided the persecutions, attacks and assassinations of our minority group. They are the ones principally responsible for having infused the masses with hatred against all Salvadoreans."[15]

The vice-consuls, who existed chiefly to try to regularize the status of Salvadorean immigrants, were especially hard hit by anti-Salvadorean activities. *El Diario de Hoy* (San Salvador), on 26 June 1969, carried a story that Remberto Aparicio, the vice-consul in Tela, had been killed by the mob when he tried to prevent their sacking his house. It added that other functionaries had been threatened.

By way of contrast, the same edition announced that in El Salvador "HONDUREÑOS RESIDENTES HÁLLANSE SIN NOVEDAD" and that the said residents lamented the violence in their own country. A declaration by these Honduran residents was also printed in which they declared that contrary to what was being reported in the Honduran press, "the people and government of El Salvador have comported themselves with great respect and cordiality." Of course, such declarations might well have been the product of fear.

During the period after the first of June, the media in both countries grew increasingly vituperative. The OAS Human Rights Subcommittee commented that "in the events which occurred in Salvador and Honduras, the press and radio bear an enormous responsibility."[16] Horror stories became more common in the Salvadorean press day by day. On 30 June *La Prensa Gráfica* reported that a Salvadorean, Gilberto Morán, was shot by the infamous Colonel Padilla in Olancho before the eyes of his wife and children. Two other children were burned to death when their cabin was set afire. The following day the paper told of the murder of a mother and her two young children, while headlines of 3 July spoke of massacres of Salvadoreans in Tegucigalpa and elsewhere, events which lost nothing in the telling and which were exaggerated.

Even notarized accounts can be fabrications, and no one knows just how many Salvadoreans in fact lost their lives; but one person which the present writer interviewed, and whom he knows to be a person of absolute integrity, went to Honduras in the midst of this crisis and there came across one individual Salvadorean who had his feet and hands chopped off by the Mancha Brava.

However widespread the violence may have been, it touched off a flood of refugees starting about 15 June and gradually building until the war itself. These pathetic people often made their way to the border with nothing more than the clothes on their backs and a few possessions wrapped in a tablecloth. On 23 June *La Prensa Gráfica* reported that 300 had arrived in

Jiquilisco from Olancho, where many had parcels of land. Another 190 arrived in Usulután, where 20 had to be hospitalized for wounds. On the next day, the paper estimated that a total of 2000 refugees had arrived and declared that aid was being organized for them in Chalatenango, Usulután, and other urban centers. General Fidel Torres, the minister of war, made an inspection trip along the border, ostensibly to investigate the refugee problem, though in the light of subsequent events, it is possible that General Torres had something more military in mind.

The notaries who took the tales of the *expulsados* heard the same tales again and again. "We were simple farmers with a few *manzanas* of land in maize and beans. All that we had was expropriated by unknown Hondurans."[17]

The burden of the refugees fell most heavily upon the Salvadorean Red Cross, which was then under the leadership of Baltasar Llort Escalante. In an interview for this work, Señor Llort said the government asked the Red Cross to handle the problem quietly, not making too much fuss. Amatillo, at the extreme western end of the country was the main crossing point, and from there the Red Cross took the refugees to San Miguel or to Santa Tecla, on the outskirts of the capital. They were kept two or three days at these relocation centers, given a medical examination and hospitalized if necessary, and received food, clothing, and money. Those who could not locate any relatives who might take them in were directed to the *alcaldías* of their home towns, where additional food and clothing were supplied, chiefly by the Church.

The question of the condition of these refugees from Honduras is a vexing one. If one believed the Salvadorean papers at the time, most of the refugees had been subjected to extremely brutal treatment; but Red Cross records, as Señor Llort pointed out, do not bear out this impression. The Salvadoreans were exhausted, disoriented, and often hungry, but they had not been harmed. A similar report appears in an article in the *Miami Herald* of 2 July 1969, in which Albert Coya reports that he had seen some two hundred refugees at San Miguel and, although dirty and tired, they showed no evidence of atrocities or mutilations.

They had all heard of atrocities, but none had seen any. He noted that no mutilation victims could be found in the hospitals of San Salvador. In the Honduran border town of Nueva Ocotepeque, Father Roderick Brennan, a North American missionary, interviewed many of the Salvadoreans who passed through on their way to El Salvador, and when I interviewed him on 21 July 1969, made much the same statement. He also cautioned against being overly credulous about what the refugees might say concerning their former wealth in Honduras, for many tended to exaggerate this, he believed, in hope of achieving a financial settlement.

Nonetheless, there were undoubtedly atrocities, as pointed out above, but these reports tend to bear out the contention that the atrocities were not so widespread as generally believed in El Salvador. The very rumor of some spectacular piece of savagery could set the population of an entire *aldea* in motion, with the Salvadorean emigrants not wishing to find out for themselves the truth or falsity of the report.

As far as the numbers of those fleeing are concerned, a letter from Chancellor Carías Castillo to the OAS on 8 July estimated that the number of Salvadoreans in his country was about 300,000, and of these 18,000 had fled back across the border.[18] The OAS Subcommittee on Human Rights speaks of a "massive exodus of Salvadoreans" and lists the number as "14,000 of all ages" who were mostly of the "modest" class of people.[19] The Red Cross in El Salvador claims to have handled some 80,000, but this total included many who fled during and after the war. Probably, by July 14 about 20,000 Salvadoreans had fled from Honduras.

During this period of tension, the diplomatic machinery which had averted war in 1967 once more came into operation. *La Prensa Gráfica* hinted on 3 May that Sánchez Hernández might again meet with López Arellano at some location along the border to talk over common problems, but the meeting never took place. On 20 June, according to the same paper, Monsignor Luis Chávez y González, the archbishop of San Salvador, made an overture to the Hondurans urging harmony. But things did not improve, and on 23 June the paper announced that authoritative sources declared that El Salvador was preparing a protest over the lack of respect for the Salvadorean consuls in Danlí and Juticalpa. In fact, Francisco José Guerrero, the Salvadorean chancellor, had dispatched on 19 June a very tough letter to Triburcio Carías Castillo. First noting the anti-Salvadorean campaign in Honduras, Guerrero declared, "My government has viewed with grave concern that one of the factors which has advanced this vandalism has been the systematic publicity campaign of various organs of information which have distorted and altered events and created other events, with all manner of injury and insult. This situation obliges me to ask the Illustrious Government of Honduras to adopt measures which law and prudence counsel." He went on to state that in El Salvador there had been no attempts against the lives or property of Hondurans. He expressed the "profound pain" of the Salvadorean people at the incidents in Honduras and added, "I am confident in the word of your Illustrious Government that it will make effective the protection of Salvadoreans resident in your Republic." The anti-Salvadorean riots he blamed upon "enemies of institutional order" trying to obstruct normal relations among the Central American peoples and the Common Market.[20]

On 24 June the Salvadorean National Assembly put forth a resolution stating that they wished to:

1. Energetically censure the outrages to which the Salvadoreans resident in the neighboring republic have been subjected.
2. Declare it lamentable that they (the Hondurans) have taken as the apparent motive to do these things the result of the recent international football games.
3. Declare that the attitude of Honduras contrasts with the serenity of the Salvadorean people in this crisis.
4. Express the desire of the Assembly and that of the Salvadorean people to see this crisis concluded in an equitable and just fashion.

The next day the Salvadorean newspapers carried a statement by Fidel Sánchez Hernández accusing the Hondurans of "violations, outrages, attacks and robberies." By then, however, the government of El Salvador had already decided upon a course of action. On the evening of 26 June 1969, Chancellor Guerrero sent to Carías Castillo the fateful message breaking off diplomatic relations between the two countries. He stated that "the government of Honduras has not taken any effective measures to punish these crimes which constitute genocide, nor has it given assurances of indemnification or reparations for the damages caused to Salvadoreans."[21]

The word of this rupture was broadcast to the Salvadorean people about eight o'clock in the evening, and in the capital even movie theaters stopped the film to make the announcement to crowds which immediately broke into wild cheers.

The next day the Hondurans, apparently taken by surprise, began to reply. Over Radio HRN, "La Voz de Honduras," the government announced: "The presidential message in which the president of the Republic ordered all civil and military authorities to guarantee the lives and property of Salvadoreans is the most ample which could be expected of responsible authority in the face of this crisis." It noted that an important meeting had taken place late the previous night in the *cancillería* to discuss the situation "created by the Government of El Salvador to provoke a kind of state of war."[22]

This ended formal contact between the two parties, and the OAS was appealed to by both sides, bringing down the aforementioned Subcommittee on Human Rights. Further, appeals were made by both parties to the other Central American states to negotiate a settlement. This does not mean that informal contacts did not continue between persons in the two governments, and a certain nostalgia for the kind of personal diplomacy that had salvaged the situation in 1967 remained. In fact, according to an important Salvadorean political leader, Sánchez Hernández called López Arellano by telephone on the very morning of the war. What he said has not been discovered, but by nightfall it was a moot question.

Chapter 7
The Hundred-Hours War

Although the political situation of Fidel Sánchez Hernández was not as serious as that of his Honduran counterpart, he was not in a completely secure position as the crisis deepened. Some modest suggestions about agrarian reform had earned him conservative opposition, and on the left the PDC was growing in importance. The government, in fact, had only a bare majority of seats in the National Assembly. Thus, when on 19 June he received a letter from José Napoleón Duarte suggesting a meeting to secure national unity, he quickly responded. On 21 June he met with Chancellor Guerrero; Dr. Humberto Guillermo Cuestas, his minister of the interior; Dr. Alfonso Rochac, the minister of economics; and Dr. Enrique Mayorga, the secretary of the presidency; as well as a host of political leaders representing virtually every noncommunist sector of Salvadorean politics. From the ruling PCN came Dr. Francisco Peña Trejo and Dr. Benjamín Interiano. The PDC sent the illustrious mayor of the capital city, José Napoleón Duarte, with Dr. Roberto Lara Velado and Julio Adolfo Rey Prendes. Their allies in the MNR were represented by Rodrigo Antonio Gamero, while the extreme right was represented by Benjamín Wilfrido Navarrete. Although the PDC leaders had been on record as opposing any military adventure, they appeared now willing to support any government action. Of the ministers present, only Alfonso Rochac bothered to suggest that any military conflict might destroy the MCCA.[1] They all declared that, whatever their political differences, they would be unified in the fact of the national crisis, and formed a Council of National Unity that met periodically during the crisis. How real this unity was would be difficult to determine. The leading luminary of the MNR, Dr. Fabio Castillo, rector of the National University, continued to speak out against

107

the government's jingoistic policies almost until the day war was declared.

The Communist Party was not invited to support government policy, nor did it. Its attitude remained much the same as it had been during the crisis of the Sleeping Beauties, when it had issued a manifesto saying that the peoples of El Salvador and Honduras "ought to realize that armed conflicts between them do not conform to their fundamental interests. . . . On the contrary, a conflict of such a nature can only aid the common enemies of our fraternal nations and retard the solution of the grave problems which confront our states."[2]

By and large, however, the populace was solidly behind the government, and was urging the government toward a confrontation. Anti-Honduran posters began to appear on the streets, some vicious, some merely funny. One labeled "Honduran Heavy Artillery" showed an elephant with several arrows protruding from his nose, while a Honduran soldier prepared to whack his testicles with a board. So great was the popular fervor that it was impossible to do even the simplest business without ending up in a protracted discussion of the refugees and their problems.

The mediation commission, made up of the chancellors of the other Central American states, met at the end of June; and on the thirtieth Fernando Lara Bustamante of Costa Rica, Dr. Alberto Fuentes Mohr of Guatemala, and Dr. Lorenzo Guerrero of Nicaragua issued a statement demanding that both governments cease whatever warlike acts or the appearance thereof which might provoke a conflict, and halt "vengeances and outrages against the dignity, life and property" of citizens of the opposing country.

The plea fell upon deaf ears, but Virgilio Gálvez Madrid, the very stiff and proper Honduran ambassador to El Salvador, declared that his government was open to suggestions. Violence, he later told me, was not the way to solve problems. Violence, however, was then beginning in earnest. El Salvador began to call up its troops on 2 July,[3] and the next day border fighting broke out. *La Prensa Gráfica* put out an extra on the third, declaring in headlines that took up the whole front page of the tabloid:

REPELIDA AGRESIÓN HONDUREÑA. The story claimed that a C-47 cargo plane and two T-28 trainers of the Honduran air force had penetrated Salvadorean airspace. Although the story did not locate the incident, it undoubtedly referred to Nueva Ocotepeque. At that town, some eight kilometers from the Salvadorean border, there is an airstrip which runs north and south. Planes taking off in a southerly direction cannot help but cross into Salvadorean airspace. Witnesses say that the C-47 was fired upon by jittery Salvadorean machine gunners as it lifted off from that strip. This was the beginning. On 5 July the paper reported another attack across the Rio Sumpal in Chalatenango at San José Olancingo. This, of course, was repulsed by heroic Salvadorean defenders, according to the press. The papers had a very marked tendency to exaggerate such incidents. Reports of 7 July spoke of "another 250,000" Salvadoreans being expelled from Honduras, when, in fact, the number could hardly have been a tenth that great.

As the border tension grew, more and more Salvadorean forces were rushed to the border; and the Central American Mediation Commission demanded their withdrawal, a demand refused on 12 July. Honduras was also asked to withdraw its troops from the border area, but did not do so, perhaps, as ex-Ambassador Gálvez claims, because there were no troops to withdraw, but more likely because the Hondurans quite rightly suspected the intentions of El Salvador. From the third on there were regular barrages of 51mm mortar fire every evening, exchanges which caused little damage but boosted the morale of the troops. These incidents were especially common along the El Poy–Nueva Ocotepeque frontier in the north.

The Hondurans, as well as the Salvadoreans, charged aggression. The Honduran Chancellery sent a telegram on 4 July to Señor Carlos Holguin, president of the Council of the OAS, listing the attack on the C-47 (DC-3) at Nueva Ocotepeque, and claiming that the plane belonged, not to the military, but to TACA, the Honduran airline. They also charged an attack on the Honduran customs post at El Poy and overflights of Honduran territory by Salvadorean aircraft.[4] All these charges appear to have been true. Those in a very good position to know have

109

stated that for at least twenty days before the incidents on the third of July, Salvadorean light aircraft, piloted by civilians who often are members of the oligarchy, had been photographing Honduran military movements deep within the boundaries of the neighboring republic.

Thirteen July saw heavier clashes than any previously reported. These were centered once again on the northern frontier at El Poy, where the Salvadorean government declared they took place "at dawn and at dusk."[5] In the wake of this fighting, Carías Castillo sent a message to his ambassador in Washington, Ricardo Midence, for release to the press, in which he announced that the Salvadoreans had fired mortars and machineguns from Rosario (in El Salvador, a few kilometers from the El Poy border) at the Cerro Cayaguanca region, north of Rosario in Honduras. He declared that six civilians had been wounded but that the "attack" had been repulsed by the Honduran counterfire.[6]

At exactly what point the Salvadoreans decided to go beyond this kind of sniping it is difficult to say. Fidel Sánchez Hernández claims that it was a last-minute decision brought about by intolerable insults and outrages, but the magnitude of the undertaking suggests a good deal of preparation. The series of aerial reconnaissance missions undertaken from mid-June on also suggest that something was afoot for some time. Sources close to the Salvadorean army claim that the plans had been maturing at least since the first of the month.

In this planning, events halfway around the world played a large part. The Salvadoreans have liked to think of themselves as the Israelis of Central America, implying that they are industrious, ambitious, technical-minded people, presumably surrounded by a lot of lazy Arabs, that is, their Central American neighbors. The 1967 "Hundred-Hours War" in which Israel knocked out her numerically superior opponents captured the imagination. Perhaps the first person to express the idea of a similar lightning attack by El Salvador was the old warrior and former President Osmín Aguirre y Salinas, who is reported to have issued a statement in June 1968, saying that in response to the threats from Honduras, "We should respond as strongly as did Israel to its 'half brother' Arabs in June 1967. If you do this,

Col. Sánchez Hernández and 75% of the patriotic Salvadoreños will be with you to the end and beyond."[7] Colonel Aguirre was drawing upon a strong popular emotion and a penchant for easy solutions, but he instinctively felt that something dramatic must be done to focus world attention upon the problems of the Salvadoreans in Honduras.

It is evident that Fidel Sánchez Hernández adopted this plan of action, but the reasons remain obscure. Juan Ramón Ardón, whose sympathies are Honduran, suggests that economic and political problems were the main considerations. He says the government of El Salvador wished to expand its territory, kill a number of Hondurans, and avoid a coup. The last, says this author, was a definite possibility because of the monopolizing of land by the oligarchy, the lack of jobs for the rapidly growing urban sector, and the "high taxes and bad laws." Ardón also cites the unrest among university and secondary-school teachers as factors causing Sánchez Hernández to undertake this "adventure." In this view there are two great bogeymen: the Salvadorean press, which inflamed sentiment, and the North American government, which wished to see "torrents of blood from hundreds of thousands of *campesino* families."[8] This view is unfair in that it does not take into account the fact that the government of El Salvador was making a deliberate response to the pressure of public opinion. In an interview with the present writer, Fidel Sánchez Hernández pointed out the great pressure he was under from public opinion and his own military, declaring that if he had not invaded on the fourteenth, there would have been a coup within twenty-four hours.

In covering the problem of war itself, it might be helpful to break it down into several questions. First of all, the historian might ask, what were the objectives of the war? Secondly, what were the tactical deployments of the war? And thirdly, how well did these operations succeed?

After extensive conversation with Fidel Sánchez Hernández, I can say that his view is that the situation with the refugees had become intolerable and that El Salvador therefore made a quick decision to attack to put pressure on Honduras to reform its anti-Salvadorean policy. He pointed out that if the Salvadoreans had wanted total victory, they would have made deep spearhead drives into Honduras, rather than entering at a number of points.

On the other hand, General José Alberto Medrano, pacing back and forth in front of the wall-length blackboard in his study, as is his custom, drew diagrams for this research in which he explained that the purpose of his former commander-in-chief was to enter Tegucigalpa in seventy-two hours. This same view is held by Luis Fuentes Rivera, who sees Sánchez Hernández as engaged in a plot to overthrow the government of López Arellano by a lightning assault toward the capital.[9]

Probably, the decision to launch a war grew out of the same impulse which led to the attempted overthrow of López Arellano during the incident of the Sleeping Beauties. Col. Fidel Sánchez Hernández was counting upon the hostility of the Liberal Party in Honduras to create an uprising coinciding, as so often had happened in the previous century, with a foreign invasion. The miscalculation lay in assuming that the Honduran politicos hated the dictator worse than they hated foreign intervention. In fact, all segments of Honduran public opinion—the unions, the opposition parties, and the middle class—rallied behind the government once the *patria* appeared to be in danger. Nothing El Salvador could say in the way of propaganda would have been able to convince even the most alienated Honduran to desert his government in the national crisis.

The claims of the former Salvadorean president that this attack was a mere punitive expedition not intended to go anywhere are not borne out by the actual tactical dispositions of the Salvadorean army. It is true that there were many border crossings by that army; but not all were of the same strength, and several appeared to have definite strategic objectives deep within Honduras.

A glance at a map of the two countries shows that there are only two major roads which connect them. One route, the more frequently used, is that which goes from the Salvadorean department of La Unión in the extreme west of the country to the Honduran department of Valle, crossing the border at El Amatillo, where there is a bridge over the Rio Goascarán. This is

the route of the Pan-American Highway. At Nacaome, Honduras, some thirty kilometers from the border, this main route joins
a branch of the Pan-American Highway which cuts north to
Tegucigalpa and from there to San Pedro Sula and the North
Coast. The distance from Nacaome to the capital is only 97 km,
over a very good road by Central American standards. The
second major route between Honduras and El Salvador is that
which leads almost due north from San Salvador into the province of Chalatenango, El Salvador. This route, designated Route
4, crosses the border at Citala into the Honduran border town of
El Poy. Eight kilometers farther north is the provincial capital of
Nueva Ocotepeque, seat of the department of Ocotepeque. From
there the road bends east along the border for some 20 km before
turning north toward Santa Rosa de Copán, which lies 78 km
from Nueva Ocotepeque. The road then begins a descent toward
San Pedro Sula, 164 km to the north. Nine kilometers short of
San Pedro, at Chamelecón, the road from Nueva Ocotepeque
feeds into the main highway from Tegucigalpa. Thus, possession
of that junction would break communications between the two
major centers and sever the capital from the North Coast. In
addition to these two main highways, the only really passable
route is that which leads north through the department of
Morazán in the northwest corner of El Salvador. It crosses the
border into the department of La Paz, Honduras, a few miles
south of the city of Marcala, and from there winds on northward
to meet the Tegucigalpa–San Pedro Sula road at Siguatepeque.
Although officially classed as an all-weather road, it could not
stand up to heavy military traffic, especially in the rainy season.

The Salvadorean army concentrated the bulk of its forces
at the two major strategic entry points. It created a Teatro de
Operaciones del Norte (TON) facing Nueva Ocotepeque and a
Teatro de Operaciones de Oriente (TOO) at the Goascarán crossing of the Pan-American Highway. There was also a force established south of Marcala in the Teatro de Operaciones Norte
Oriental (TONO) and a minor theater of operations in Chalatenango known as TOCH. From this it can be seen that the object,
if all went well, was to create a pair of giant thrusts which would
close upon the two major centers of Honduras like ice tongs.

Anything in between these two was designed to draw off elements of the undermanned Honduran army.[10] This sort of enveloping action was what the Salvadoreans admired in the campaigns of Israel against the Arabs; but as it turned out, it was one thing to make such maneuvers with tanks over a desert and quite another to make them by truck and jeep through the mountains and jungle-filled valleys of Honduras.

Another major factor in the victories of Israel had been the swift air strikes which had neutralized the air forces of the Arab countries. The Salvadorean air force prepared to make similar attacks, but it was woefully lacking in equipment and training, despite the presence of a North American Military Advisory and Assistance Group which had been working intensively with the air force for some time, as had a similar group in Honduras. El Salvador had only eleven combat planes, all propeller-driven ships dating from the Second World War—F-51 Mustangs and F4-U Corsairs. There were also five DC-3 transports and some light aircraft. Honduras, which had the advantage of a superior group of pilots, had twenty-three combat aircraft, mostly Corsairs which had been received between 1956 and 1960.[11] There was really only one airfield in El Salvador from which military strikes could be launched, the international airport of Ilopango just west of the capital, while Honduras had a number of good airfields, including the two international airports that served Tegucigalpa and San Pedro Sula. These factors made the task of the Salvadorean air force a difficult, if not a hopeless, one.

The Salvadoreans decided to overcome the enemy's advantage in equipment and training by launching a preemptive strike. It would take off from Ilopango at 1750 hours and be over Toncontín Airport by 1810 hours. In addition strikes would be made simultaneously at Nueva Ocotepeque, Santa Rosa, San Pedro Sula, Nacaome, and several other airfields. The evening hour was chosen, as General Medrano explained it, because it would be too late for the Honduran air force, which lacked sophisticated navigational equipment, to respond before darkness fell. Because of the number of targets, the Salvadorean attack force had to be spread very thin; and to make up for the lack of combat aircraft, the DC-3s were pressed into service as

114

"bombers," with external racks being provided. The chance of actually hitting something from a lumbering transport without bomb sights was most remote, but the plan was carried out more for the psychological effect of having two-engine bombers than out of expectation of practical results.

Fourteen July being D-Day, the pilots assembled at 1500 hours for a briefing. The planes were secretly armed at the military compound, about half a mile from the Ilopango terminal building; and they began to taxi out about 1730. Everything that could go wrong did go wrong. Two planes collided on the runway. The squadron commander leading the attack on Toncontín failed to find it in broad daylight, a feat accomplished daily by commercial airliners. Separated from his squadron, this captain ultimately landed his craft at Guatemala City, to the astonishment of local authorities.

The Honduran air force, which had been carefully spread at a number of locations, was virtually undamaged by the attack; but the sight of enemy war planes over the capital in an undeclared war aroused public opinion to a fever pitch. To continue the story of the air war, the next morning the Hondurans scrambled together everything that would fly and descended on El Salvador. Virtually no preparations had been made to cope with this eventuality other than to have some of the fighters in the air. A confused and inconclusive dogfight took place over the capital for our early-morning amusement. Ilopango was bombed; but outside of a couple of pits in the runway, no damage was done. However, very serious damage was done at the ports of La Unión and Acajutla, where the oil storage tanks were set afire. These blazed throughout the war, and the columns of thick black smoke could be seen from forty miles away.

Col. Enrique Soto Cano, the commander of the Honduran air force, had prepared his pilots for aerial combat; and one of them became an instant national hero. This was Major Fernando Soto, who, cruising in his Corsair on the sixteenth, shot down three Salvadorean fighter planes over Nacaome and Goascarán. Lieutenant Vladimir Varela and Captain Reynaldo Cortez, known affectionately to the North American advisers as "Crazy Cortez," were killed in that action.[12]

If Honduras had it all its own way in the air, the much more important war on the ground was destined to go the other way, though perhaps not as much the other way as El Salvador might have liked. For this war El Salvador could muster a much larger force than could Honduras. There were some 8,000 well-trained men in the regular army, and a large group of reserves which could have been brought in had the fighting continued. Further, about 1,000 troops were drawn from the security forces, mostly from the elite Guardia Nacional along with several hundred Policía Nacional used mostly for garrison duties, as in the captured town of Nueva Ocotepeque. For these operations the police units put on the combat fatigues of the regular army, but kept their customary weapons. The Salvadoreans also had a number of 105mm artillery pieces, but no tanks that worked. The Hondurans, on the other hand, had only about 2,500 troops in the beginning, plus various security forces and but a single battery of artillery.[13] To make things even worse for them, the Hondurans had no rifle better than the old M-1s which had been supplied by the United States, while the Salvadorean army and Guardia had recently been reequipped with German-made automatic rifles.

Not only was the Honduran army lacking in arms and equipment, but it was ill organized and filled with corruption. Various cliques of officers struggled for control, including extreme rightist "gorillas," neutralists (in the internal political struggle), and "petit bourgeois revolutionaries" who opposed López Arellano.[14] The army was also bitterly at odds with the Cuerpo Especial de Seguridad which also took part in the war.

The Northern Theater of Operations was the scene of some of the bloodiest fighting of the war. TON was under the command of Col. Mario de Jesús Velásquez of the regular Salvadorean army, but also operating in TON was an independent force under Gen. José Alberto "Chele" Medrano, made up entirely of crack troops of the Guardia. These forces were scheduled to jump off at 0500 hours on the fifteenth, after a night of mortar and light artillery fire. Colonel Velásquez's units consisted of the First Battalion under Major Alirio Hulgo and the Eighth under Col. Ernesto A. Claramount Rozeville. A third unit, the "Tigres

116

del Norte" was a smaller, commando-type organization. The First Battalion was to storm directly across the border along the main road to Nueva Ocotepeque, while Colonel Claramount's unit on the right made its way through the foothills from Cerro Cayaguanca to Cerro la Chicotera, which overlooks Nueva Ocotepeque. The Rio Lempa cuts north just to the east of the city's airport, and the "Tigres" were to march up the east bank of the river and cross it at the Nueva Ocotepeque airport, which they would then seize. The Guardia column, of about battalion strength (some seven-hundred men), was to attack from Las Pilas, ten kilometers to the east of the main assault. This attack was designed to take advantage of the fact that the Nueva Ocotepeque–Santa Rosa de Copán road bends eastward eight kilometers from the border and thus could be cut beyond Nueva Ocotepeque by this column if they could make their way over the torturous mountain trails with only mule and horse transport.[15]

The thrust of Colonel Velásquez went according to plan. The Honduran force of less than a thousand was concentrated along the road just south of the airport and some six kilometers deep in Honduran territory. The forces holding the hills west of the city were weak and were easily brushed aside by the strong advance of Colonel Claramount, who thus outflanked the Honduran troops in the valley and had a clear field of fire upon them. It was, in fact, pretty much of a massacre, with the Salvadoreans suffering only light casualties. Nueva Ocotepeque was siezed on the evening of the fifteenth; and by noon the next day the whole area was secured, except for snipers on the surrounding peaks, who would continue to be active until the twenty-first. After the seizure of the provisional capital, Velásquez's force pushed on toward La Labor.

It was at this point that the expectation of a rapid advance broke down. The Honduran Ranger Battalion, crack troops under Colonel Arnaldo Alvarado, held the road beyond Nueva Ocotepeque, with their headquarters at La Labor and advanced units holding the hilltops around El Morral. The narrow macadam road winds through these jungle-covered hills with many excellent places for an ambush. The drive slowed and halted some eight or ten kilometers from the

117

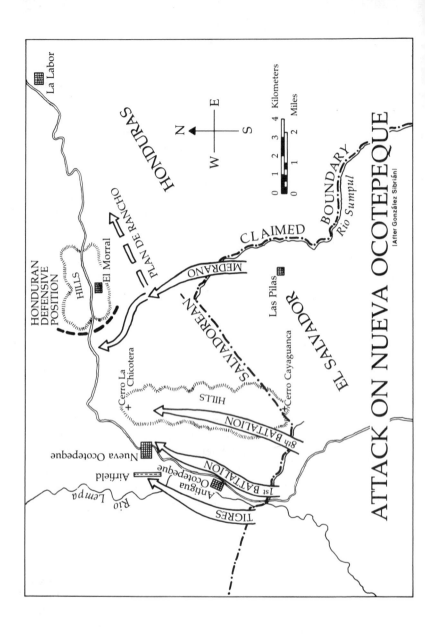

ATTACK ON NUEVA OCOTEPEQUE

(After González Sibrián)

118

captured city. This problem should have been solved by the thrust of General Medrano from Las Pilas, but Medrano lacked adequate maps of the area; trails did not go where they were supposed to, and there was virtually no coordination between Medrano and Velásquez. Medrano appears to have gotten lost at one point, but he eventually found himself at Plan de Rancho, due west of Nueva Ocotepeque, from which he dispatched a force under Capt. Aristides Napoleón Montes toward El Morral. If his force had arrived in back of El Morral, the road might have been cleared, but they joined the main thrust short of that objective and were likewise stalled. In the meantime the main column of General Medrano was cutting its way through the tangled ravines and heavily wooded hills toward La Labor. They never arrived and with the truce fell back on Plan del Rancho. Although the penetration of some fifteen kilometers was very respectable, considering the terrain, the actions on the TON never came up to the hopes of the Salvadoreans.

Nueva Ocotepeque, a provincial capital of some five-thousand inhabitants, was the largest city over which the invading forces gained complete control. It is a clean-looking town, arranged on the typical Spanish American gridiron pattern with a large central square, where two years earlier the Sleeping Beauties had meekly surrendered. On one side of the square lay the administrative offices of the department and the *alcaldía*; on the other was the church, run by two Capuchin missionaries from the United States. As the Salvadorean army approached the town, the inhabitants, fearing rape and pillage, had hastily evacuated by truck, tractor, horse, and mule, heading over the road which led to Esquipulas in Guatemala; for the border was only eighteen kilometers away. Some hundred unfortunates who had not made good their escape took refuge in the church hall, where they were under the care of the missionaries.

When I arrived there on the afternoon of 19 July, the town appeared deserted, except for the company of Policía Nacional camped in the *alcaldía*. The church compound across the deserted square was "protected" by a huge United States flag draped over the wall. This was the idea of Father Roderick Brennan, the remaining Capuchin (his partner, Father Walsh, had become shell-shocked during the bombardment of the town and was evacuated to San Salvador), who thought that the symbol might deter anyone trying to molest his refugees in the church. In this he was very much mistaken. A certain Colonel Návez appeared the next morning and rounded up the unfortunate Hondurans. He told them that no harm would come to them if they left the church compound and that the Salvadoreans were their friends. They viewed this with some suspicion as one youth out foraging had been shot and a girl who had left the compound had been raped by two soldiers. When Father Brennan was asked by the colonel to agree with his words, the priest stoutly refused, and as a result, a short while later he was arrested in his own parish house as a Honduran spy. He was roughed up considerably, interrogated, and sent to San Salvador, where he was later released and sent to Guatemala. The fate of his remaining parishioners has not been learned.

Certainly, what happened to Nueva Ocotepeque represents in miniature the whole tragedy of the war. Father Brennan remarked that most of those who fled to Guatemala would never return, and indeed by the time the war was over, there was very little to return to. The inhabitants of Nueva Ocotepeque joined tens of thousands of their fellow countrymen as war refugees. When one adds to this group the eighty thousand Salvadoreans chased from Honduras in 1969, it is easy to see that there was an enormous dispossession of individuals, either temporary or permanent.

On the nineteenth a theoretical cease-fire was in effect, but in actuality there was considerable gunfire to be heard all around the town. This kept up through the night of the nineteenth-twentieth and only slackened off about midday on the twentieth. By the next day the cease-fire appeared to have held.

In Nueva Ocotepeque this writer talked to a Salvadorean officer, Lieutenant Antonio Palacios, who explained to me the soldier's view of what the war was all about. He said: "I am a poor man, the son of a peasant. . . . When Martínez, *the* Martínez, came to our village . . . he liked my father and gave him jobs to do. 'Boys,' my father said, 'when you grow up that's the profession! Be soldiers.' My brother is a soldier too. But I never want to kill anybody. In the *campo* we love life. . . . But we didn't start this war. El Salvador is a small country with little money, a small army. Why would we want a war? This war will ruin us. We don't dislike Honduras. Many of my friends are officers in the Honduran army. We trained together in Panamá. Now if I meet them I have to shoot them. . . . But what are we to do? Honduras is driving our people out, raping little girls, cutting off breasts, cutting the balls off men. We didn't start this but now we must fight. . . . This town is ours now and we'll keep it. I am a soldier and I am willing to die here. I don't want to die, but I will for my country."[16]

The eastern front was on a broader scale than the attack on Nueva Ocotepeque. This was partly owing to the fact that there were more and better roads in this area, particularly the main route of the Pan-American Highway, which crossed from El Amatillo to a point just south of Goascarán on a bridge over the river of the same name. There were several other points where the river could be crossed in order to link up with all-weather roads on the Honduran side. From Goascarán the road ran straight to Nacaome, about thirty kilometers distant. Once this latter point fell and the river beyond it was crossed, the Nicaraguan border and the department of Choluteca would be cut off from the interior of Honduras.

There were several attacks in the TOO. The Eleventh Battalion, backed by the bulk of the Salvadorean artillery, was to storm over the Goascarán bridge and directly along the Pan-American Highway toward Nacaome. In a move reminiscent of the actions of the Eighth Battalion at Nueva Ocotepeque, the Fourth was to cross at the same point and then cut north through the hills to Langue, so that it could cover the highway from the foothills. Part of this battalion was also to swing north and take Goascarán. Some twenty kilometers farther north, the Fifth Battalion was to cross the river and seize Aramecina and then follow a secondary road deep into the department of La Paz. South of the Pan-American Highway a small group of Special Forces was to cross the river and seize Alianza, then strike northwest to the Pan-American Highway. Much farther south, the Sixth Battalion, under Colonel Benjamín Mejía, was to seize the islands in the Gulf of Fonseca. The Tenth Battalion at Santa Rosa de Lima was to be the reserve. The whole force was under the command of Gen. Guillermo Segundo Martínez, the artillery under Maj. Joaquín Evelio Flores Amaya. It is worth noting that both Benjamín Mejía and Flores Amaya would be involved in the abortive coup of 1972.

Like the attack at Nueva Ocotepeque, this one began well only to run out of steam. Aramecina, Goascarán, Alianza, were all quickly captured as the Honduran army fell back to defensive positions around Langue and before Nacaome. The islands in the gulf were also overrun. Initially, the power of the Salvadorean 105mm howitzers and the presence of hastily constructed armored personnel-carriers proved too much for the Hondurans. The Hondurans themselves had little artillery, few old 75mm howitzers, and their individual weapons were inferior. But as the war moved deeper into Honduran territory, the lack of ammunition of both sides slowed the proceedings. The invaders advanced a maximum of twenty-five kilometers along the Pan-American Highway and did not take Nacaome.

The only other significant penetrations of the war, those in TONO into La Paz, along the Marcala road, and of TOCH from Chalatenango into the department of Lempira, likewise failed to make any really deep penetration.

The Organization of American States and, especially, the United States government were gravely alarmed over the outbreak of hostilities. Efforts were underway on the morning of the fifteenth to arrange a cease-fire, and the OAS appointed Dr. Guillermo Sevilla Sacasa of Nicaragua to the chairman of a peace commission which went to each of the warring states. At the same time special representatives from both sides appeared before the OAS Council in Washington on the evening of the sixteenth. Roberto Perdomo, the former chancellor of Honduras, denounced the large-scale invasion, while Dr. Alfredo Martínez Moreno, president of El Salvador's Supreme Court, raised the question of genocide. Ambassadors Julio Adalberto Rivera of El Salvador and Ricardo Midence of Honduras were also present at the OAS Council meeting. To this Council meeting the United States sent Joseph J. Jova, just home from four years as

THE EASTERN FRONT
(After González Sibrián)

5th BATTALION → Aramecina

N
W — E
S

0   5   10 Kilometers
0 2   4   6 Miles

Pan American Highway
Santa Rosa de Lima

4th BATTALION → Langue
Goascorán

11th BATTALION

EL SALVADOR

El Amarillo

SPECIAL FORCES

Pan American Highway
To Nacaome →

HONDURAS

Río Goascorán

La Unión
6th BATTALION → ZACATILLO

GULF OF FONSECA

EL TIGRE

MEANGUERE

ambassador to Honduras,[17] a move which, rightly or wrongly, the Salvadoreans did not take as a friendly one on the part of the Nixon administration. Sevilla Sacasa had arrived in San Salvador on the evening of the fifteenth, accompanied by John Ford (United States representative), Jorge Fernández (Ecuador), and Raúl Quijano (Argentina). They began to shuttle back and forth between the capitals in a DC-3, an act not without a certain amount of heroism considering that many trigger-happy fighter pilots were in the air. By the evening of the seventeenth, Sevilla Sacasa was able to report to Tiburcio Carías Castillo that El Salvador had accepted the proposals of the OAS. The actual cease-fire went into effect at 2200 hours on the night of Friday, 18 July 1969. It was, however, very slow to take effect; and not until midday on Sunday, 20 July, did the guns actually become silent.

The OAS observers arrived in the respective capitals on the nineteenth, and on Sunday morning, the twentieth, they began at 0500 hours to move to their respective positions. These observers came from the United States, Argentina, Ecuador, Nicaragua, Guatemala, the Dominican Republic, and Costa Rica, care having been taken to get as broad a sampling of OAS states involved as possible, including the other Central American nations.

Public opinion in San Salvador was definitely not behind these peacemaking moves. *El Diario de Hoy* carried banner headlines on the eighteenth, declaring, "No Cease Fire without Reparations." The article which followed declared that El Salvador would never withdraw its troops without guarantees of compensation for the Salvadorean victims of Honduran expulsions. Because of the strength of this feeling, the occupying troops made no immediate plans for withdrawal.

On the twenty-first a spokesman of the Foreign Ministry of El Salvador declared that "there will be no withdrawal without guarantees of Salvadoreans living in Honduras. That is the official position of the government."[18] Handbills began to appear, declaring, "We Will Get Out of Honduras When the USA and Russia Get Out of Germany," and other, similar, messages.

Faced with this problem, Galo Plaza Lasso went to the Salvadorean embassy in Washington on the night of 28 July and advised Rivera that the General Commission of the OAS would take up three resolutions, the first two of which would condemn El Salvador for violating the Treaty of Rio and levy sanctions against that country, as well as promising aid for Honduras. The third resolution would state that if El Salvador were to withdraw her troops, the OAS would assure respect for life, personal security, and property for those nationals in each other's countries.[19]

The Salvadorean leadership was now in a very difficult position. Francisco José Guerrero announced publicly that the OAS would have to condemn Honduras for genocide before El Salvador would withdraw.[20] Looking back on these events from the perspective of nine years, Col. Fidel Sánchez Hernández considered that the real problem was not so much any declaration from the OAS as the fear of what would happen to the remaining two-hundred-thousand Salvadoreans in Honduras. "We did not want to withdraw the troops, despite the pressure, until we felt that the rights of Salvadoreans were secure," he declared.

But the pressure was now too strong and so, taking the third resolution as a kind of moral victory despite the condemnation by the OAS of the invasion, El Salvador agreed late on the night of 29 July to withdraw its troops. Sevilla Sacasa and his group worked out the details of this withdrawal on the next morning, and by the second of August the army had come home. They received a heroes' welcome, and a great national victory celebration was proclaimed, with a parade on 5 August in which easily half a million people took part as either participants or spectators. It took half the day to move the entire parade through the downtown streets of San Salvador and out along the Avenida Roosevelt past the reviewing stand where Sánchez Hernández; General Fidel Torres, his war minister; and other dignitaries were gathered. Later, a great monument was put up in one of the finest streets of the capital to *los heroes*, the fallen warriors of the Hundred-Hours War.

Before moving on to questions concerning the period after the war, there are several points which might be taken up. One of them concerns the number of those actually killed in the war. Earlier, the figure of 3,000 from Jiménez was cited. William Durham speaks of "several thousand dead on both sides,"[21] while the *New York Times*, on 16 July 1969, headlined "Heavy Casualties." In the same vein many eyewitnesses put the number of those killed very high, with Colonel Flores Amaya declaring that he did not think the figure of 5,000 any too great. On the other hand, *Newsweek* placed top estimates of those killed in the fighting at around 500 on either side (28 July 1969). José Luis González Sibrián, in his rather careful book, lists a total of only 107 Salvadorean military killed, including a corporal and seven privates of the Guardia. This pretty well coincides with Colonel Lovo Castelar's total on Guardia, as he lists one lieutenant, a corporal, and seven privates killed.[22] I would therefore accept the figure of 107 as being fairly accurate. Juan Ramón Ardón declares that 99 Hondurans were killed in combat and 66 wounded.[23] In all, perhaps 250 combat troops were killed. But the number of casualties among civilians and irregular guerrillas and militia is much harder to determine. It seems to me not unlikely that as many as 2,000 people in all lost their lives in this conflict, which does not make this a major war by any standard. The figure of 2,000 killed is also given by the *New York Times*, 23 December 1973.

Another problem is raised by the charges and counter-charges of atrocities during the war. Armies are by nature atrocious, and Central American armies lack nothing in this regard. At the thirteenth inter-American conference of foreign ministers, held at the OAS headquarters on 26 July, the Hondurans persuaded the group to look into charges of atrocities by Salvadorean troops, despite the presence of some twenty Salvadorean pickets outside the building, demanding justice for their countrymen in Honduras.[24] Baltasar Llort, the head of the Salvadorean Red Cross at that time, denies any maltreatment of the civilian population or of prisoners of war during this period. He declares that even those left behind in Nueva Ocotepeque were well treated by the military. He admits, however, that those

Hondurans captured in the invasion who were of military age were sent along to the prisoner-of-war camp in San Vicente along with those taken in combat. Just how large a number the latter might have been is not known, but the Salvadorean White Paper speaks of 253 being brought to San Salvador on the sixteenth.[25] The Hondurans likewise rounded up a great many Salvadoreans in their country, without much regard to age, though they appear to have taken mostly males. Señor Mejía Pardo, a prominent Honduran journalist, tells me that many of these were lodged in the National Stadium, where the first soccer game of the series had been played, under what he describes as very bad conditions, with little food or drink. As the stadium was, and is, open to the sky, and this was the rainy season, one can well guess that conditions were not the best. The *New York Times*, 17 August 1969, claimed that 8,965 Salvadoreans were still detained in Honduras, while 238 Hondurans were in Salvadorean custody. On the whole, considering the pitch to which tempers had been raised, it is surprising that there were no wholesale massacres on either side. Perhaps it is true, as Durham suggests,[26] that the common people did not always share the hostilities of the upper classes.

Still another question that keeps resurfacing in interviews is the degree of involvement by the United States in the war. On one level it is quite clear that the two sides were using North American equipment against each other. Senator J. William Fulbright, chairman of the Senate Foreign Relations Committee, said he was embarrassed by the warfare "to the degree that we have responsibility. They might have solved it with fists and feet if we had not furnished them the arms to use instead." To this the United States secretary of defense, Melvin R. Laird, responded that the aid to these countries was "a very small amount."[27] Fulbright was correct in raising the question of the wisdom of arming these small states, which could use the arms only on each other or upon their own peoples, but Laird was right in saying that the amount of military hardware and training contributed by the United States was small; and it seems likely that if the United States had refused to contribute such aid, it might have been obtained from other sources, even without going to the communist world.

It is also curious to speculate on the roles of the Military Advisory and Assistance Groups in each country. Colonel Flores Amaya has told me that he believes that the American advisers knew all about the plan to invade Honduras; but for this once only I must say that I would tend to disagree, although there is no definite proof either way. If the high-ranking advisers interviewed by this writer at the time of the conflict really knew what was planned, they must have been candidates for Academy Awards, for never did any group appear more startled.

Indirect aid is another question. The gossipy Thomas McCann states in his book on the United Fruit Company that a "former high-ranking official in the United States Department of Defense" was advising El Salvador on its public relations during the war. On the other hand, he tells us that UFCO provided money to send United States journalists to Honduras to promote the Honduran side of the story, and that he himself thoughtfully advised the Hondurans to put Russian-made weapons in the hands of dead Salvadoreans in order to sway North American opinion, a tactic which, he adds, had worked so well in Guatemala.[28] Certainly, as the propaganda by Joseph E. Maleady in El Salvador attests, private individuals from the United States chose sides in the conflict; but there is no evidence of any overt North American pressure for either side before the invasion, when, understandably, the United States pressured El Salvador to withdraw from the occupied territories in conformity with the Treaty of Rio de Janeiro.

The aftermath of the war would spin many legends of battlefield heroism and ferocity, some of them true, but most of them highly exaggerated. The real tragedy of the conflict should be seen not simply in terms of what went on in battle, but rather as part of a massive disruption in the lives of simple peasants from both countries. This army of the dispossessed and up-rooted was greatly augmented by the events of July 1969, and the progress of both nations greatly hindered.

Chapter 8
A Decade of Tension

From the strictly juridical point of view, Honduras was in a strong position before the Organization of American States and world opinion. Whatever actions had been taken against the Salvadorean immigrants were taken within her own borders, against persons who were, in any event, not legally resident; for less than 1 per cent of the Salvadoreans had the required legal documents.[1] On the other hand, the Salvadorean invasion appeared as a direct challenge to the international order. Article 17 of the OAS charter states: "The territory of a state is inviolable; it may not be the object of military occupation or of other means of force taken by another state, directly or indirectly, whatever the motive, even temporarily. Acquisitions of territory or special advantages which are obtained by force or by whatever means of coercion will not be recognized." Article 7 of the Inter-American Treaty of Mutual Assistance declares that in cases of armed conflict the *status quo ante bellum* must be restored. These articles were the basis of Tiburcio Carías Castillo's appeal to the OAS.

The Hondurans wished to look at the situation from a legalistic point of view and to ignore the very real provocations which had been offered to El Salvador. The Salvadoreans themselves believed that they had a strong case for claiming that they were in the right. Not only was Dr. Alfredo Martínez Moreno dispatched to Washington to aid ex-President Julio Rivera in pleading the Salvadorean cause, but an all-party commission was organized and dispatched to the headquarters of the OAS. This was under the leadership of Renaldo Galindo Pohl and included Abraham Rodríguez of the PDC, the writer José María Méndez, the conservative Wilfredo Navaret, and several others. According to Dr. Méndez, they found the atmosphere in Washington very hostile to El Salvador. Frank Aguirre, the State

Department representative with whom they met, appeared to be totally unconcerned with the plight of the Salvadoreans in Honduras and only interested in the aggression of El Salvador. One temporary result of this was the solidification of all shades of political opinion behind Sánchez Hernández. Upon their return to San Salvador, Rodríguez and Méndez proposed that an all-party government be established to express the solidarity of the entire community in the crisis. The plan fell through, with the PDC blaming the PCN and vice versa, but it did indicate that external hostility had produced a nationalist sentiment which certainly did not hurt the popularity of Sánchez Hernández.

Honduras approached the conferences in Washington with considerable confidence. In his instructions to the delegates to the OAS meeting, Chancellor Carías Castillo told them that he had no doubt that El Salvador would be branded the aggressor; but if the OAS should show any tendency to shrink from openly condemning her, they should present their case "dramatically, if you will, pathetically,"[2] instructions which they followed to the letter. Indeed, the level of bombast on both sides attained considerable heights.

His counterpart, the foreign minister of El Salvador, Francisco José Guerrero, in an address which he had read before the second plenary session on 30 July 1969, declared that he had been betrayed and tricked into permitting the withdrawal of troops. "When I informed you of the withdrawal of Salvadorean troops, I stated that the government of El Salvador put its trust in the foreign ministers (of Central America) that they would be able to find formulas to guarantee fully and effectively the lives, security and goods of the Salvadoreans who reside or did reside in Honduras."[3] But no such result had been forthcoming; and the persecutions, so he declared, went right on. These complaints he reiterated in a note to the Investigatory Commission of the OAS, dated 22 August 1969. He stated that "in contrast to this spirit (of good will) and attitude of serenity and respect and devotion to peace and tranquility demonstrated by the Government and People of my country, the Government and People of Honduras have continued aggressions against El Salvador."

He then listed several points: the continued existence of what he styled concentration camps, holding some fifteen thousand Salvadoreans; the propaganda emanating from HRN, the national radio of Honduras, and the newspapers; terrorism and the boycotting of Salvadoreans. He called Honduran cooperation with the peace resolution of the OAS "a joke," and urged the OAS again to see to it that human rights were respected.[4]

In more florid style Ambassador Rivera spoke before the thirteenth reunion of foreign ministers of the OAS, declaring that El Salvador had listened "with holy stoicism, for holy is our cause," to "falsehoods and calumny" from Honduras.[5] While the rhetoric of such pronouncements might have been inflated, it should be noted that from 14 July to the end of the year the number of refugees reached a total of some sixty thousand, a fourth of all the Salvadoreans in Honduras.[6] Something was causing the massive exodus to continue. A memorandum in Salvadorean files, written in November 1969, noted that the situation in Honduras remained tense, and that while the government of Honduras was itself not persecuting Salvadoreans, it was allowing private individuals to do so.

One immediate result of the conflict had been the sealing of the border between the two countries. Actually, El Salvador had taken the first step in that direction in early July when it closed its border in a vain attempt to stem the flow of refugees, but it was now Honduras which was adamant that the border remain closed. The reason was not simply pique over the invasion, but rather that Honduras had long suffered from an influx of Salvadorean goods under the Common Market. As soon as the war was over, Honduras demanded a revision of the MCCA. Eddy Jiménez correctly points out that this was a logical move to reestablish protective measures.[7] Efforts in July 1970 at the foreign ministers' meeting in Managua were unsuccessful. The Honduran legislature then made protection an official policy on 31 December 1970, when it adopted a resolution to separate the country from the MCCA and authorized the Chancellery to effect bilateral treaties with other Central American states. Chancellor Carías Castillo pointed out at this time that even after the break with El Salvador, the trade deficit with the Central American States had been L76,100,000 for 1970. Costa Rica, likewise an unhappy partner in the Common Market, also opened bilateral talks with Nicaragua and El Salvador, as well as with Honduras.[8]

César A. Batres, who succeeded Carías as chancellor, in discussing this matter, conceded to me that Honduras would never, under any circumstances, take back the old Common Market as it was before the war. Although the war initially hurt the economy of the country, his feeling was that "Honduras has obtained an economic advantage from the war and is no longer tied to Salvadorean products." He pointed out that Honduran world exports in the mid seventies have more than made up for the loss of exports within the Common Market. There would be no practical advantage from a return to the MCCA. Nevertheless, he pointed out, in the long run there must be economic cooperation among the Central American states for the development of the entire region. In fact, a Normalization Commission was set up to revamp the MCCA, but it made little advance.

The decline of the Common Market was hurting the trade of El Salvador. *La Prensa Gráfica*, 13 March 1975, noted that sales to MCCA countries decreased 7 per cent in value in 1970, and although these sales then rose 9 per cent in value in 1971, 12 per cent in 1972, and 18 per cent in 1973, they showed a smaller cumulative increase than Salvadorean trade as a whole.

At the end of January 1970, the tension along the border again erupted into large-scale fighting. Honduras claimed that Salvadorean planes bombed two villages, and a border town in Honduras was attacked by a force of one hundred Salvadorean troops. In a second clash on 5 February, four Salvadorean troops were reported killed. These incidents led to renewed negotiation. In Washington the OAS brought together Ambassadors Rivera and Perdomo, but the OAS talks collapsed at the end of May. The Central American foreign ministers met in San José, Costa Rica, 2–4 June 1970, and under the urging of President José Figueres of Costa Rica, came up with a plan accepted by the hostile parties. This Pact of San José was designed to defuse border tensions by agreeing that neither of the two countries would have naval patrols in the Gulf of Fonseca and by establishing a three-kilometer "zone of security" on either side of the border from which all but local police would be withdrawn. President Figueres praised both sides for their cooperation, and a turning point in negotiations appeared to have been reached. All this was well and good if everyone could agree where the border was, but that was precisely the problem. The San José plan was forced to provide "special dispositions" for such disputed areas as the zone of Sabanetas, just southwest of Marcala, Honduras (much of it occupied by the Salvadoreans), and for the area Las Tablas-Sazalapa (Arcatao).[9] Little of this was immediately implemented, for neither side could agree on the specifics. Thus, a new meeting was scheduled for 20 May 1971 to make proposals on reopening telephone communications and the Pan-American Highway, while an agreement between Honduras and El Salvador reestablished postal and telegraph service in August 1970.[10]

Before the May talks could open, there were several violent clashes at the end of April, in which, according to the *New York Times*, 1 May 1971, a Honduran soldier was killed at Las Tablas. The OAS then dispatched a force of twenty officers from eleven Latin American states to patrol the border. Despite the friction created by renewed killings, the various lines of communication were at least partly opened in May. Shortly thereafter, on 6 June, Ramón Cruz was inaugurated as the new president of Honduras with a pledge to continue working through the OAS for settlement.

The government of El Salvador was also destined to change hands soon, Sánchez Hernández having engineered the election of Arturo Armando Molina of the PCN to succeed him on 1 July, 1972. Both countries, therefore, pressed for a settlement that would become effective before the new government took over. Unfortunately, the very able Francisco José Guerrero had been forced out as chancellor in the maneuvering for the presidency, resigning in October 1971. This meant that negotiations had to begin with fresh faces at the table, for Carías Castillo had also given way to César A. Batres as foreign minister of Honduras.

A discussion between the two Chancelleries took place on 11 June 1972, in which the Hondurans proposed a general treaty

be signed, including a definition of *los limites*. To secure a definition of these frontiers, a mixed commission was proposed. But
although the foreign ministers seemed to agree in these informal
talks, the governments delayed the process.[11]

Negotiations got down to a firmer footing when Foreign
Minister Batres took the initiative before the thirteenth meeting
of OAS foreign ministers. Chancellor Batres stated that he was
in accord with the statement of his Salvadorean counterpart,
Mauricio Borgonovo Pohl, that the lack of success of previous
negotiations was owing to the fact that they were always on an
informal basis which then could not be translated into treaty
texts. He suggested that the time had come to make formal
proposals before an international body for a treaty of peace. He
then met secretly with Borgonovo Pohl, and they came up with
eight points for negotiation: 1) the text of a peace treaty, 2) free
transit between countries, 3) counsular and diplomatic relations,
4) frontiers, 5) the Common Market, 6) claims for damages and
other differences, 7) human rights and family reunification, and
8) general dispositions. They further agreed to meet on 15 September 1973.[12]

But the ultimate effect of all this was more frustration, with
the talks breaking down in late December. It was the position of
Borgonovo Pohl that matters should be handled in a flexible
manner, with such simple matters as free transit being handled
first. He pointed out to the Special Commission of the OAS in
April of 1973 that El Salvador was already allowing Hondurans
free passage in and out of his country, and he proposed that
Honduras reciprocate and then move to establish diplomatic
relations. The real problem, he held, was "the inflexible attitude
of the Government of Honduras, in its insistence that the diverse
aspects of the general problems form a whole of parts necessarily
inter-dependent."[13] From this so-called inflexible position Batres
had not budged.

The toughest nut to crack, and the one which Honduras
insisted had to be cracked in order to arrive at a solution, was
that of the boundary line. But no adequate demarcation survey
exists, although there are excellent aerial maps of the border
region, including the one which covers two whole walls in the

office of Salvadorean negotiator Arturo Castrillo Hidalgo. Essentially, there are six *bolsones,* or pockets of territory, over which the two countries cannot agree. Jorge Fidel Durón, former Honduran head of the mixed commission on boundaries, listed these as Goascarán, 57.0 square kilometers; Dolores, 54.08 square kilometers; Naguatereque, 148.4 square kilometers; Sazalapa, 51.0 square kilometers; Cayauanca, 38.1 square kilometers; and Tepanguisir, 70.3 square kilometers—a total of 419.6 square kilometers. Castrillo Hidalgo lists the areas somewhat differently, as Citala—El Poy, Las Pilas (both south of Nueva Ocotepeque), Arcatao (Sazalapa), Sabanetas, Monteca (Dolores), and the region south of Goascarán, much of it swamp extending out into the Gulf of Fonseca, and including the islands of the gulf. However one approaches it, the issue is a touchy one. Although in some areas El Salvador has been in possession only since the war, other areas, such as Hacienda Dolores, have been long-standing trouble spots that have produced such incidents as the Martínez Argueta affair in 1967.

Over the years of dispute, the Salvadoreans have declared, as Mauricio Borgonovo did on 12 December 1973, that El Salvador has never had any designs upon Honduran territory. On the other hand, there is Article 8 of the Salvadorean Constitution, which declares that "the territory of the Republic within its present limits is irreducible." This limits Salvadorean negotiators because although no one is sure what *is* Salvadorean territory, they do not have any guarantee that some future Salvadorean government might not decide that they had indeed bargained away national territory and thus violated the Constitution. In his interesting book on the question, the distinguished Honduran jurist H. Roberto Herrera Cáceres declares that "the notion of irreducibility has no common usage in the field of international public law; its value, in consequence, is limited to the field of Salvadorean internal law."[14] This might be cold comfort to Salvadorean negotiators. Honduran law also prohibits secession of national territory, although this is not a constitutional provision.

At issue here is a question of priorities. From the Honduran point of view, the border issue is *the* issue. Vice-chancellor Poli carpo Callejos, who has long been a permanent fixture in Hon-

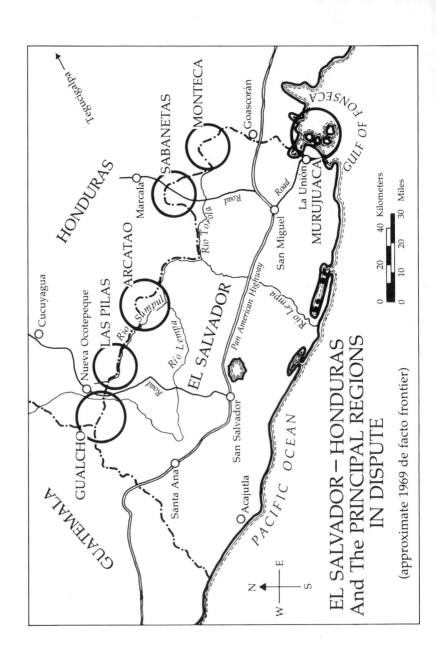

EL SALVADOR–HONDURAS
And The PRINCIPAL REGIONS
IN DISPUTE

(approximate 1969 de facto frontier)

duran foreign policy, declared to me that "our position is that the border is the major source of friction between the two countries." He pointed out that the other boundaries of Honduras have been fixed, and that in each case Honduras accepted the award, whether favorable or unfavorable. Similarly, Jorge Fidel Durón declared that he could see no reason why a border settlement could not be easily reached. "We have met in San José, Managua, Washington and all over the map," he said and expressed his opinion that El Salvador was dragging its feet.

The Salvadorean position is that the war was caused by the expulsion of refugees, not by the undefined frontier, and that Honduras is making an issue of this one question to prolong negotiations. The Salvadoreans point out that any final agreement would restore some form of the Common Market and would allow a new influx of Salvadoreans into Honduras, neither of which that country can tolerate. If Honduras really wants to solve the border issue, volunteered Castrillo Hidalgo, he would be glad to put on his hiking boots and survey the whole terrain with some competent Honduran and find the border by simply asking each person they met whether they were in Honduras or El Salvador! Really at stake is a question of pride. Before the war Honduras had schools, a hospital, and a garrison at Sazalapa. Now Arcatao flies the Salvadorean flag, as does Dolores and other places in which Honduras has an emotional investment.

As long as the conflict continues, there will continue to be border incidents. In December of 1973, there was shooting along the border; but the then defense minister of El Salvador, Col. Carlos Humberto Romero, denied any serious armed conflict was going on and characterized the affair as "routine maneuvers." Almost seven years to the day after the start of the 1969 war, on 13 July 1976, the shooting again broke in earnest in the Sazalapa region and near Hacienda Dolores. The violence of this incident alarmed both sides, and the respective chancellors met in Guatemala with President Kjell Laugerud on 29 July. That very day there was another border clash. Mauricio Borgonovo Pohl declared that his government had every intention of abiding by the accords of San José reached in 1970, but both sides felt that a more firm agreement needed to be made.[15] This point was underlined on 1 August, at a moment when OAS peace-keeping units were on their way to the border. Roberto Palma Gálvez, who had replaced Batres in October 1972, declared that El Salvador had attacked no less than six border towns.

The result was a meeting which took place in Managua during August 1976, leading on the ninth to the Act of Managua. This provided for the following: 1) the accords of San José would be confirmed with regard to the stationing of observers along the frontier; 2) there would be a definitive settlement of the boundary; 3) there would be compliance with the San José accords in regard to the location of troops (for no troops were supposed to be stationed directly along the border); 4) areas of conflict would be free of troops; 5) areas of conflict would be free of paramilitary forces (having in mind such organizations as ORDEN in El Salvador); 6) security forces would retire to their bases; 7) the clash areas would be under observers; 8) displaced civilians would be allowed to return to the border area; and 9) the accord would be accompanied by a detailed protocol.

Even then there were problems. The Honduran representative to these talks, Lt. Col. César Elvir Sierra, insisted that it be noted that actions toward the definitive solution of the differences on boundaries between Honduras and El Salvador would be initiated within the pertinent machinery of the OAS. This bothered Gen. Armando Leonidas Rojas, the Salvadorean representative, who signed with the reservation that this "was completely alien to the Accord of San José."[16] Since that time a kind of "shuttle diplomacy" has been in effect.[17] But the difference between the Salvadorean desire for a piecemeal solution and the Honduran insistence on "universal and simultaneous solutions to all problems" continued, at the end of 1979, to impede the progress of negotiation.

A prominent Honduran journalist confided to me in the summer of 1978 that the people of Honduras were tired of all this and would like a solution, and that the press felt the same way and would welcome any solution. *La Tribuna,* 31 July 1978, expressed optimism on the state of negotiations, but quoted

Andrés Víctor Artiles, head of the union CTH, as warning that "a solution must not lead to the re-importation of foreign labor as many are currently out of work in Honduras."

At the end of the decade, it was possible for Hondurans to move freely in and out of El Salvador, either by car, by bus (for there is regular bus service by a Costa Rican firm between Tegucigalpa and San Salvador), or by air (through Guatemala City, for there is no direct air link). On the other hand, Salvadoreans resident in Honduras might freely leave; but no Salvadorean, including those formerly resident, could recross the border into Honduras. Again, while Salvadorean goods cannot be imported into Honduras, many of them make their way in disguised as Guatemalan products. As many families have been separated by the conflict, it has been necessary for the Red Cross of the two countries to work closely together in cases of family emergencies. Patients from Honduras are sometimes brought to medical facilities in El Salvador.

In 1978 it was decided that a third-party mediator ought to be chosen; and the choice fell on the former Peruvian president José Luis Bustamante, a man of advanced years. Cynics suggested that the choice was deliberately made in the hope that the mediator would die before negotiations could be concluded, so that more time could be lost in selecting a new mediator. While this is hardly the case, it would certainly tax the energy and stamina of any negotiator to reconcile the differences between the two parties.

Changes in the foreign ministries of both countries did little to improve matters. In Honduras, in July 1979, the government of General Paz García replaced the well-informed Foreign Minister Roberto Palma Gálvez with Eliseo Pérez Cadalso, regarded by many as anti-Salvadorean. Across the border the revolutionary junta in October of that same year replaced Foreign Minister Rodríguez Porth with the very able academician, Héctor Dada.

Both countries also continue to experience internal problems, with those of El Salvador becoming worse than those of her more backward neighbor.

139

Chapter 9
El Salvador: Coming Apart

For months after the war, the refugees continued to stream across the border, on foot and in trucks and buses. Some of them were pathetic and disoriented, some defiant and resentful; all of them left desperately poor. The *New York Times* reported on 11 November 1969 that 61,000 had come across the border since the end of the war, and another estimate gives 81,105 by the end of December with 16,585 more expected by March 1970.[1] In all probably 130,000 Salvadoreans eventually returned.

The country they returned to could hardly have welcomed them. After the trash and dead flowers were cleaned up from the "victory" parade, people began to realize that there had been no victory at all and that the country had lost much more than it had gained in a few glorious hours of combat. The lucrative Honduran markets were gone, and a general disruption of trade had taken place. There were, in addition to the refugees, who were little more than a drop in the ocean,[2] daily more mouths to feed from the natural increase of the population which would double the number of Salvadoreans by 1980. By 1971 unemployment, total and hopeless, claimed 20 per cent of the country's work force, while another 40 per cent were underemployed, working no more than 120 days a year. Rural evictions continued as the press toward cash crops, as opposed to subsistence farming, went on in the countryside; and those evicted drifted into La Fosa and the other shanty communities around San Salvador. The government, distressed at the visible poverty on the streets of the capital and anxious to aid the permanent merchant community, added to the woes of the urban poor by getting rid of street peddlers and attempting to destroy the shanties.[3]

The concentration of wealth and especially wealth in land continued to increase after the war. By 1975 8 per cent of the

141

population controlled 50 per cent of the total wealth of the country, while 58 per cent of the people earned no more than $9.60 a month. Of the rural population, a mere 7 per cent had aggrandized 81.3 per cent of the total land. In terms of arable land, the concentration was even more pronounced, with 2 per cent of all farms owning 56.5 per cent of the total.[4] While wages remained low, prices were rising at 60 per cent a year.

The problems of El Salvador in the seventies were of such magnitude that a drastic change in leadership seem inevitable; but the PCN in fact showed a remarkable talent for holding on to the reins of power, if not a talent for solving the problems of the country. The municipal and legislative elections of 1970 had even seen the PCN dramatically increase its share of the government, through the usual methods of force and fraud in rural areas.

Returning from Washington, Reinaldo Galindo Pohl had proposed that an all-party cabinet be formed as the first step toward moving the country toward democracy, but the ruling clique of army officers rejected this move. They further denied Galindo Pohl the nomination for the presidency in the contest of 1972, preferring to stick with a military man. The most obvious military man for the post was General José Alberto Medrano, whose tough Guardia Nacional provided the muscle that kept the regime in power; but Medrano had made many enemies, not only because of his reputation for personal ferocity but also because of his flamboyant private campaign during the 1969 war. He was dismissed as chief of the Guardia, and ran into legal difficulties in 1971. The choice of the military and the PCN turned out to be the colorless Col. Arturo Armando Molina, a close friend of Sánchez Hernández who could be relied on to carry out his policies, which were to support the landed oligarchy and keep democracy under wraps.

The opposition forces, however, still believed that they could wrest control from the PCN in an election, even though it might be one tainted with fraud. Previously, the PDC and the left-wing parties had campaigned individually and backed separate candidates; now, however, they decided to meet the ruling party as a unit. A Unión Nacional Opositora (UNO) was formed of the PDC, the Unión Democrática Nacionalista (UDN), and the Movimiento Nacional Revolucionario (MNR). The UDN was widely regarded as a front for the illegal Communist Party of El Salvador, while the MNR was made up chiefly of university intellectuals, such as ex-rector Fabio Castillo, who had been the candidate of the old Partido Acción Renovadora in the 1967 presidential election.

The UNO offered the ruling clique its first real challenge since 1961 and at a time when the fortunes of the government, thanks to the collapse of the MCCA, were very low. To make matters worse for the rulers of El Salvador, the UNO came up with an exciting and dynamic candidate, José Napoleón Duarte, the Christian Democratic mayor of San Salvador and the most popular political figure in the country.

In the election of 20 February 1972, there were two other candidates besides Duarte and Molina. One was "Chele" Medrano, representing a small splinter group from the PCN; and the other was José Antonio Rodríguez Porth of the extremely right-wing Partido Popular Salvadoreño. Neither of these candidates was taken seriously. Duarte was another story. The early returns from San Salvador and other urban centers put him clearly ahead in the race. Something had to be done, and it was, in rural areas beyond the scrutiny of poll watchers from the opposition. The final count put Molina in the lead by a hundred thousand votes; but because it was a four-way race, he did not have the absolute majority of votes required by the Constitution, which presented no problem, as the Assembly was controlled by the PCN and duly certified Molina the winner. It had been a scare for the colonels, and one they had no desire of repeating. The next presidential election, that of 1977, would be fraudulent from the very beginning.

If ballots could not unseat the PCN, perhaps bullets could. There were a number of officers who were disenchanted with the regime, and they found a leader in Colonel Benjamín Mejía, who had been a front-line commander in the 1969 war. This group of younger officers fit into the persistent pattern of Salvadorean politics since the Second World War. Just as younger, more progressive officers had unseated Casteneda and substituted Oscar Osorio, and just as Lemus had been turned out and replaced by Rivera, so might Sánchez Hernández be toppled before he could turn over power to Colonel Molina on 1 July. After talking with members of this group, it is my impression that what they wanted was not free elections and democracy, but rather a more efficient government in which, of course, they would themselves have a piece of the action. Only at the last moment did they realize the need to broaden their base and make contact with Duarte, Castillo, and the other political leaders of the opposition. This, as one of them later admitted, was a major blunder.

At first the coup went swimmingly. Sánchez Hernández was seized at the presidential palace by troops from the neighboring barracks of El Zapote. Across the country commanders pronounced for the new regime, but too soon; for the forces of the PCN rallied. There was then bitter street fighting in the capital and some two hundred persons were killed, with many more being wounded.[5] At last Mejía released the president and surrendered to loyal commanders. For once the normal pattern of Salvadorean politics had failed to repeat itself.

In a society which lacks faith in democratic principles, the coup can be a progressive force. Each time a regime's corruption reaches a certain level, the regime can be replaced by a disaffected group ready to test their own incorruptibility. But the PCN grimly hung on, despite its manifest corruption and incompetence, and things simply became worse. Sánchez Hernández and Molina now knew who their enemies were and had a good chance at cleaning house. Prominent persons compromised by the coup could now be exiled, and this list included such threats to the regime as Duarte and Fabio Castillo. They remained outside the country until the coup of October 1979; and they were joined, following the election disturbances of 1977, by a whole new bunch of exiles. And while Eddy Jiménez's claims, that twenty-five people a day were executed in the months following the abortive coup, are somewhat exaggerated, it is still true that the government did use the incident as a pretext for martial law and for getting rid of a number of undesirable persons in the army, the unions, and in politics. The repression was heaviest in the eastern zone and especially in the department of San Miguel.[6]

For El Salvador 1972 was one of those great historical turning points the true significance of which lay precisely in the fact that history had failed to turn on schedule. The fraudulent election and unsuccessful coup produced a general disillusion and disenchantment with the two "normal" methods of effecting change. This mood would be accentuated by the legislative and municipal elections of March 1974, in which the PCN used a great deal of coercion to gain an almost total victory.

But in the period between the two elections, a novel method of exerting political pressure had begun to assert itself: guerrilla terrorism. The movement began in the summer of 1973, when a group of four left-wing guerrilla fighters robbed the Bank of London and Montreal in central San Salvador. This was followed by an incredibly bold stroke on 24 November, as revolutionaries sealed off a downtown street in the capital and calmly proceeded to rob a gun store of fifty pistols and automatic weapons. Three persons were also killed by the guerrillas in this attack, which took place only a couple of blocks from the headquarters of the Policía.

There were actually several groups of terrorists in the field. One was the Ejército Revolucionario Popular (ERP), which, in the beginning, had links to the Communist Party. In May 1975 the ERP underwent a great internal upheaval when a dissident group attempted to take over the organization and murdered Roque Dalton García, the famous communist poet and intellectual who had been the ringleader of the ERP. After that the ERP severed all connections with the "bourgeois" Communist Party. The chief rival of the ERP was the Fuerzas Populares de Liberación (FPL), also known as the "Farabundo Martí Brigade," and representing an extremely radical Marxist sect. There was also a group known as the Organización Revolucionario de Trabajadores (ORT) and one called the Frente Nacional de Liberación (FNL). Indeed, for a while these organizations appeared to spring up almost monthly. Some of them were nothing more than a few thugs more interested in profits than in the proletariat, and some were, no doubt, actually people in the pay of the

145

police who used the cover of revolutionary terrorism to inflict private vengeances, but others were genuine revolutionaries.

Assassinations and kidnappings soon became frequent. In April 1974 the FPL shot and killed the secretary of the presidency, Raymondo Pineda Rodrigo. Prominent members of the oligarchy also suffered. The ERP attempted to kidnap Rodolfo Dutriz, of the family that ran *La Prensa Gráfica,* in September 1975 and wounded him in the fray. The FPL did kidnap and later ransom Benjamín Sol Millet early in 1976. Two major assassinations of 1977 were those of Foreign Minister Mauricio Borgonovo Pohl, after he had been kidnapped by the FPL in April, and that of Colonel Osmín Aguirre y Salinas, the ex-president. Both of these seemed particularly senseless in that Colonel Aguirre was eighty-three and a threat to no one, while Chancellor Borgonovo Pohl was an outstanding public servant and one of the most decent figures in the regime. The rector of the National University was also killed in September. This perhaps made better sense in revolutionary terms; for the university, following the unsuccessful coup in 1972, had been placed under direct government control, and the rector was hated by the students for his repressive tactics. In 1978 the focus of guerrilla activity shifted away from political figures toward the members of the international business community. A Japanese industrialist was kidnapped and later found murdered, while two British businessmen were kidnapped for ransom. In 1979 the same pattern continued.[7]

While the government was not directly threatened by the terrorism of the extreme left, it was deeply embarrassed. Tourists shunned the strife-torn country, and foreign capital became increasingly reluctant to invest. But every plan the government made for improving the image of El Salvador seemed to end in disaster. In July of 1975 the country played host to the grotesque "Miss Universe" pageant, spending 1.5 million dollars on it at a time when people were dying of hunger on the streets of the capital. The opposition had a field day with this, and on 30 July there were massive demonstrations which resulted in a good deal of killing by the security forces. Another scandal was the arrest and subsequent conviction in the United States of the chief of staff of the Salvadorean army, Col. Manuel Alfonso Rodríguez, on gunrunning charges. He may well have been set up by colleagues who wanted him out of the way. A second fraudulent legislative and municipal election in March of 1976 also contributed to harming the image of the government, especially since the ruling PCN generously awarded itself every single seat in the legislature and every mayorship in the country. Seeing this new fraud shaping up, the UNO had tried to withdraw its candidates from the races, to leave the PCN with a hollow victory. "If they tried that in a fascist regime," said President Molina, "they would be forced to participate in the election." A few days later he denied them permission to withdraw their candidates.[8]

While politics stagnated and terrorism grew, the basic problems of the country remained unsolved. Although there was some foreign industrial investment, such as that of the Japanese textile firms and Texas Instruments from the United States, these firms employed a very small amount of labor in their highly mechanized and computerized plants. If the vast majority of Salvadoreans were to be employed, they would have to be employed in the countryside; but here the pattern of substituting cash crops for food crops and of illegal enclosures by the *hacendados* continued unabated.

In the aftermath of the war, there had been growing pressure for agrarian reform. A national agrarian reform conference had been held in January 1970 with representatives of all factions. The conference had called for land expropriation with compensation and an end to the ban on peasant unions. This had, however, frightened the landed oligarchy, who clung with a feral tenacity to their lands and privileges; and they succeeded in blocking any attempt to turn the recommendation into legislation.

In the early seventies, seeing the desperate situation of rural El Salvador and anxious to help, the United States government and the AF of L–CIO had sent the American Institute of Free Labor Development (AIFLD) into the country to organize the peasant. AIFLD encountered a number of problems, partially because of its reputation as an alleged CIA front, and partially due to the heavy-handed tactics of its agents. It eventually with-drew from El Salvador, but it did encourage the formation of the first significant *campesino* organization, the Unión Comunal Salvadoreña (UCS). Although farm-worker unions were specifically illegal in El Salvador, the government tended to encourage UCS for fear of getting something worse should it fail. And UCS also sought to work with the government. Through the intermediary of a sympathetic army officer, UCS approached the government in 1976 with the proposition that Molina might still have their support and could abandon election frauds if he would consent to some form of land reform. The result of this was that in June 1976 President Molina announced a land reform scheme.

The land reform scheme of 1976 was to be carried out through the Instituto Salvadoreño de Transformación Agraria (ISTA), which had been founded the previous year. Fifty-nine thousand hectares in the littoral which had previously been cotton land, would be developed into peasant communities with the aid of UCS.[9] This was really no more than a pilot project, a trial balloon, in fact, to test the atmosphere for land reform.

If President Molina wondered what the oligarchy would think of this, he soon found out. Opposition quickly surfaced from the Asociación Nacional de la Empresa Privada (ANEP) and from FARO, which is actually two organizations, the agri-cultural federations of the eastern and western regions. FARO mobilized landholders in the cotton region, holding armed meet-ings, refusing to sell land to the government, and resisting ex-propriation. ANEP was able to mobilize the entire strength of the private sector against the government's proposal, which it maintained was unconstitutional and ill conceived. In its annual report ANEP declared that "the fundamental point in the contro-versy about the agrarian problem we consider to be this: whether El Salvador will go on being a nation in which free enterprise is respected, or whether, on the contrary, it will change itself into a directed state."[10]

In discussing the views of ANEP, Ernesto Rivas Gallont, the suave financier who often acts as ANEP's spokesman, ex-plained to me that his organization had no objections to the peasants getting land. Let them take out loans like anyone else,

148

he suggested, and buy the land at the market value so that they would understand the value of money and the importance of hard work. This kind of land reform he could certainly back. These Goldwaterite views, and rumbling from within the military, caused a quick change of direction by President Molina. By October 1976 the land reform scheme was dead, and so was any hope of *campesino* support for the regime.

The peasants were starting new organizations and finding new allies. Two powerful *campesino* groups now arose to challenge the more timid UCS. These were the Unión de Trabajadores del Campo (UTC) and the FECCAS, the Christian peasant movement encouraged by some of the Catholic clergy. These organizations were in fact illegal and were not awarded legal standing *(personería jurídica)*, an excuse that the government used in persecuting them, although it should be pointed out that FARO did not have legal standing either.[11] Together, UTC and FECCAS with other organizations form the Bloque Popular Revolucionario (BPR). The Bloque believes in militant, direct popular action and is quite hostile to the government. There is also the Frente de Acción Popular Unida (FAPU), made up of a number of peasant groups and left-wing unions.

In January 1977 the peasant movement found an unexpected and very powerful ally when the aged Archbishop Chávez of San Salvador retired to be replaced by Monsignor Oscar Arnulfo Romero. A short, squarely built, stolid little cleric with a determined set of the jaw, Monsignor Romero was adamant that the social-justice doctrines of the Church, which had played such a large part at the Medellín, Colombia, meeting of the Latin American bishops in 1968, would be implemented in El Salvador. He encouraged the "liberation theology" of much of the younger clergy and made his weekly sermons from the National Cathedral an occasion for protest against the poverty and backwardness of his country. At first some of the other bishops appeared to go along, but as things grew desperate, they followed the cue of the papal nuncio and withdrew their support from the position of Monsignor Romero. To many of the people of El Salvador he remained a national hero, and over a hundred members of the British Parliament put his name in nomination for the Nobel Peace Prize for 1979, a move in which they were joined by several members of the United States Congress.

The militant attitudes of the Bloque, FAPU, and the archbishop, led to many confrontations. In these the government had the benefit not only of the regular security forces but also of a network of other organizations. These included ANEP and FARO, but more importantly the Organización Democrática Nacionalista (ORDEN). ORDEN was the brainchild of "Chele" Medrano, back when he was head of the Guardia, and its great growth was in the period when Gen. Carlos Humberto Romero had charge of it as minister of war. ORDEN was designed as a patriotic society, working closely with the army reserve, the security forces, and conservative elements to maintain order in the countryside and to track down subversives. There were a good many privileges that went with being an ORDEN man, including the right to pack a pistol without any official permission, a crack at government jobs, and the ability to violate the law with impunity as long as one cooperated with local security forces. Some eighty thousand people were enrolled in ORDEN, but the number of activists was much smaller. ORDEN did not have *personería jurídica,* but of course was never bothered on this account. While ORDEN operated openly, a shadowy group of right-wing terrorists also existed, the Unión Guerrera Blanca (UGB), which was rumored to be under the direction of the Policía Nacional and to be composed largely of ex-police officers. It engaged in assassinations and other terrorist activities and maintained links to such groups as the Mano Blanca, its Guatemalan counterpart.

Major clashes between peasant groups on one side and the security forces and ORDEN on the other had been the rule since November 1974, when there was a massacre of peasants at Cayetana which sparked a wave a bombings against government installations by the ERP and FPL.[12] The center of confrontation was the region just north of the capital city. On the road between Aguilares and El Paisnal in the department of San Salvador, Father Rutilio Grande, S.J., was shot down from ambush by members of the UGB. This was on 12 March 1977 and was owing to the fact that Father Grande had emerged as a leader of the peasant community. In protest at this murder, the archbishop had all the churches of the country closed, except for the cathedral, where he celebrated a commemorative mass attended by over one hundred thousand people. On May 17 two thousand army troops and Guardia, aided by ORDEN, stormed the Aguilares area. They evicted peasants from lands they had been sharecropping around Paisnal and shot down fifty peasants "in cold blood." Hundreds more were arrested and of these many simply "disappeared" forever, while others were released after torture.[13] On the day before the invasion of Aguilares, a diocesan priest, Father Alfonso Navarro, was murdered by the UGB in San Salvador because of his radical views.

Shortly before the Aguilares invasion, the country had been treated to a presidential election. The candidate of the PCN was the former minister of war, Gen. Carlos Humberto Romero, while the UNO, with its major leaders all in exile, decided to go with a hero of the 1969 war, Col. Ernesto Claramount Rozeville. The government planned this election as carefully as a military campaign, hooking up the PCN forces throughout the country by shortwave radio in order to assure that their candidate had the majority. During the balloting of 20 February 1977, such cryptic messages emerged from PCN headquarters as "put more sugar in the urn than coffee"—that meant to stuff a few more votes into the voting urn for General Romero. They ended up with plenty of sugar, but the opposition was not ready to take this supinely. A massive demonstration took place for a week in downtown San Salvador at the Plaza Libertad (the traditional gathering point for protesters). Finally, on 28 February the government massed thousands of ORDEN volunteers and security forces, who savagely attacked the square, killing an estimated two hundred. Colonel Claramount and some of his followers took sanctuary in the nearby cathedral, only to be routed out and arrested. Claramount then joined Duarte, Castillo, and the rest of the exile community. The government tried to hide the extent of the massacre, announcing that two or three person had been killed in political disturbances, but eyewitness accounts speak of bodies being thrown into the open sewers and of pools

151

of blood washed away with fire hoses. The president-elect was clearly serving notice that he meant business.

But the government now began to feel the weight of international displeasure, especially that of the United States, where human rights had become a political issue. To make matters worse, the Salvadorean government was now accused of killing a North American ne'er-do-well by the name of James Ronald Richardson, who had been picked up twice in San Salvador on minor drug charges. The second time, he joined the ranks of those permanently disappeared; and blame was laid by the Americans on Colonel René Chacón, the director of immigration and ex-officio head of the secret police. United States Ambassador Ignacio Lozano pressed these charges vigorously and in general complained of the quality of human rights. When James E. Carter became president, he accepted the resignation of Lozano, a Republican, and replaced him with professional diplomat Frank Devine, who operated in a lower key; but the incident refused to go away. Chacón himself was soon beyond shedding any light on the subject. Dismissed by Romero, he was gunned down in his car on the streets of the capital in January 1978, probably by those who felt he knew too much.

Because of the persistence of peasant unrest and guerrilla terrorism, the new president, who had taken office on 1 July 1977, decided that a stringent new law would be necessary. This is the *ley de orden*, of 24 November 1977. In effect the "law of order" set up a modified permanent state of seige, setting penalties for those who might "propagate, promote or make use of their personal status or position to spread doctrines. . . that tend to destroy the social order or the political and juridical organization established by the Political Constitution." It also penalized those who "participate as members in any organization that maintains doctrines which are anarchic or contrary to democracy," and those who "spread at home or send abroad, by word of mouth, writing or by any other means, false or tendentious news or information destined to disturb the constitutional legal order."[14] With such a sweeping law President Romero could take action against virtually anyone for anything. The law was repealed in the spring of 1979.

The election massacre, the invasion of Aguilares and El Paisnal, and the *ley de orden* now brought down upon the government two human rights missions from abroad. One was from the OAS and was made up of lawyers from four participating countries; the other was an unofficial mission headed by Congressman Robert Drinan of the United States; and both arrived in January 1978. Plainly worried about its image abroad, the government of El Salvador did its best to cooperate with both of these investigations. President Romero, in his conversation with Congressman Drinan (who is himself a Jesuit priest), laid heavy emphasis on the fact that since he had assumed office, no priests had been exiled from the country.[15] However, after he made that statement, five more priests were killed in 1978 and 1979.

A new major clash also occurred in late March of 1978 when ORDEN supporters tangled with members of the Bloque at San Pedro Perulapán, twenty kilometers northeast of San Salvador. The army stepped in on 27 March, invading San Pedro Perulapán itself and the surrounding *cantones*. The Associated Press reported twenty nine persons killed in this action. Sixty-two residents of the area were arrested. The Bloque, to win their release, occupied five foreign embassies in San Salvador on 13 April, stating that their purpose was to force an amnesty. These events prompted President Carter to dispatch the deputy assistant secretary of state for human rights, Mark Schneider, to San Salvador for a week's investigation.[16] In short, the transfer of power from Molina to Romero did little to ease the situation which one observer characterized as "the people versus the government.[17] Romero differed from his predecessor chiefly in being more inept and more ruthless.

Under these circumstances the situation grew increasingly ominous. The BPR, led by Facundo Guardado, now associated itself with the terrorist FPL, while FAPU formed a close connection with the terrorist group known as the Fuerzas Armadas de Resistencia Nacional (FARN). These developments meant that the terrorists were no longer isolated, but rather could count on the support of the mass organizations of peasants and workers, the BPR alone having an estimated sixty thousand members. This was much the same thing that happened in Nicaragua, where terrorism had given way to civil war by 1979. Encouraged by the Nicaraguan events, the popular forces became more bold.

The increasing impotence of the government was seen in the seizure of a number of embassies, public buildings, and churches. In January 1979 FAPU seized the Mexican embassy and the headquarters of the Red Cross. Responding to the arrest of Facundo Guardado, the BPR seized the cathedral of San Salvador on 4 May, along with the French and Venezuelan embassies. Although Guardado was released, the seizures led to violence. A taunting crowd of BPR suppporters on the cathedral steps were ruthlessly shot down by the Policía on 8 May, and on the twenty-third a group of women and children bringing fresh supplies to the captors of the Venezuelan embassy were machine-gunned on the street outside the building. A total of thirty-seven Bloque supporters lost their lives in these clashes.

The kidnappings, assassinations, and bombings by the ERP, FPL, FARN, and other groups reached a new high in September 1979, encouraged by the fall of Somoza in Nicaragua. The country appeared on the verge of civil war when two aspiring colonels, Adolfo Arnoldo Majano and Jaime Abdul Gutiérrez, seized power from General Romero, who was sent into exile (on 15 October) following the coup. The colonels soon formed a junta composed of themselves, automobile dealer Mario Andino, Guillermo Ungo of the MNR, and Román Mayorga Quirós, formerly rector of the Catholic Universidad Centro-americana (UCA). The inclusion of these last two brought hope for sweeping reforms, while the appointment as foreign minister of Héctor Dada, formerly head of the economics department at UCA, raised hopes of a speedy settlement with Honduras.

The success of the junta should have been secured by doing two almost impossible tasks: disarming the right-wingers in the army and security forces and at the same time bringing an end to left-wing terrorism. The junta became known as the *junta da Chompipes*, that is, the junta of the Christmas turkeys, because it would be plucked, cooked, and eaten by that date. As it turned out, it was cooked and served up by its own members, not for Christmas, but for New Year's, because it utterly failed the test of leadership. After that, a second junta was formed in which the very able

Héctor Dada was moved from the Foreign Ministry to become a member. This group had a slim chance of bringing the country under control.

The question remains as to how far the social and political deterioration of El Salvador over the last decade has been the product of the Soccer War, but certainly this much can be said: the war removed a major safety valve from a potentially explosive situation. For many thousands who might never have emigrated to Honduras, the option was still open. Since the closing of this exit route, attempts to establish similar emigration patterns to Guatemala have met with considerable resistance, not only from the Guatemalan government but from anti-Salvadorean terrorist groups linked with repressive right-wing forces. Migration to the United States has also become very popular, as the immense queues outside the United States embassy attest but this route requires more funds than the average Salvadorean can hope to possess. The war and the break with Honduras have therefore made a significant contribution to the feeling of desperation that still grips the country. It might be further pointed out that the war ultimately damaged the prestige of the government and the military. At first the reaction of the country was one of praise for both these institutions, and there is no denying that the army performed well on the field of battle. But as the negotiations dragged on, it became apparent that more had been lost than gained in this rash venture. In particular the destruction of the MCCA has worked to the disadvantage of El Salvador, producing the shutdown of factories, unemployment, and insolvency.[18]

For a time during the mid-seventies, world coffee prices tended to boost the Salvadorean economy, but since 1977 those prices have begun to fall. Román Mayorga speculated in an interview we had before the coup that if coffee prices were to fall drastically, "another 1932 might be the result." These ideas are echoed by William Durham in his highly informative study.[19]

Alexis de Tocqueville observed long ago that the most dangerous time for a government is when it tries to remedy longstanding abuses. The junta certainly appears sincere in its desires for reform, but the crisis of El Salvador remains unresolved.

Chapter 10
Honduras: Progress and Problems

On Thursday, 3 August 1978, I met with César Batres in the green pastel presidential palace with its battlements and medieval turrets in downtown Tegucigalpa. The secretary of the presidency outlined for me the plans which President Juan Alberto Mélgar Castro had for the future of the country. On Monday, 7 August 1978, at 9:30 P.M., the government of Mélgar Castro was overthrown, and César Batres dismissed from office. *Tegucigolpe* was running true to form.

But underneath the apparent instability of Honduras, there was a certain amount of progress being made. Hondurans, a happy-go-lucky people, are used to seeing presidents made and unmade and feel that a good deal of their personal liberty, which they prize so highly, is the result of political chaos. Since the 1969 war they had witnessed a number of political upheavals.

One result of the war had been that Oswaldo López Arellano was largely discredited, for if El Salvador had not really won the war, Honduras clearly appeared to have lost it. Whatever ambitions the swashbuckling air force commander might have had to be a new Carías Andino were dashed by the fiasco of 1969, and his military associates made it clear that he ought not try to extend his governance beyond the legal five-year limit. The problem was to revive politics and parties long dormant under the military regime. The Nationals were easiest to get back into the lists as they had close ties to the regime; the Liberals were harder to corral; but in the end a compromise was worked out in which the election for the presidency would be truly contested between the two parties, and the representation in the Legislative Assembly would be divided equally in advance of the election with each party getting half of the sixty-four seats in the Assembly. The speaker of the Assembly would be from the

National Party, while the president of the Supreme Court would be a Liberal.

This was to be a direct election contest by popular vote, the first since 1932. In the elections since that time, the Assembly had in fact chosen the president. So little faith was had in these proceedings that only about one half of the nine hundred thousand potential voters bothered to turn out for the March 1971 contest. In the end the National candidate, Ramón Ernesto Cruz, was declared to have won a narrow victory over the Liberal Jorge Buezo Arias, who had been minister of economics under Villeda Morales. In fact the contest was probably orchestrated to attain the desired result, with López Arellano moving behind the scenes. In the new government López Arellano remained the chief of the armed forces, which gave him a virtual veto over all acts of President Cruz. It soon became apparent that he did not like what he saw. Rigoberto Sandoval was dismissed by Cruz as head of the INA, and a "go-slow" approach was taken toward land reform. The pact between the Nationals and the Liberals also broke down, and the two establishment parties began openly feuding. The result was that on 3 December 1972, after Cruz had been in office a scant twenty months, López Arellano overthrew his regime through a bloodless military uprising, taking care to cover his own tracks by being out of the country at the time.[1]

One major reason for the failure of the Cruz government was the poor performance of the Honduran economy. In the three-year span from 1970 to 1973, the gross national product rose by only a 6.2 per cent total; and while in 1972 exports rose by 18 per cent, imports increased 37 per cent in value.[2] It should be further noted that since 80 per cent of all exports are by foreign-owned firms, the full benefit of such exports is not felt by the national economy.[3]

Part of this poor economic performance was due to the disruption of the war. Leiva comments that the price of the war "was very high, but the war had, all the same, positive results."[4] These positive results began to assert themselves in the second administration of López Arellano. Substitute industries began to replace Salvadorean imports, and new exports were developed, such as sugar. Sugar had been exported until 1928, when Cuban sugar had forced Honduras out of the market, but in the mid-seventies Honduras again found herself able to sell this product to other Central American states.[5]

The coup not only brought a renewal of prosperity, it further stimulated the growth of unions and of land reform. The INA had lain dormant during the Cruz presidency, but now it shook off its lethargy and began to move. Decree 8 of the new government enabled it to force landholders to rent underutilized portions of their holdings. It further led to the establishment of some five hundred peasant settlements, largely on former estates. In January of 1975, López Arellano initiated a new land reform act, Decree 170. This act was designed to distribute six hundred thousand hectares among 120,000 families over the space of five years. It also set limits by region on the maximum size of landholdings, and all these were less than five hundred hectares. Lands which would be expropriated by the INA under this system would be paid for in agricultural bonds.[6] The great disaster which had occurred on 19–20 September 1974, Hurricane Fifi, which destroyed some 60 per cent of the country's agricultural production, actually aided in the implementation of the law; for many landholders were not reluctant to part with some of their devastated lands. The influential newsletter from London, *Latin America*, declared that the new agrarian reform law was "the most significant development in a decade" (17 January 1975). It was a "brave and bold course" in a country where 75 per cent of the peasantry were either landless or had less than six hectares.

It was one thing to decree land reform; it was another thing to enforce it. FENAGH, the Honduran counterpart to FARO in El Salvador, bitterly resisted the law, but in Honduras the peasantry were far better organized than in El Salvador. The Unión Nacional de Campesinos made itself very active. On 19 May 1975 the UNC invaded 120 haciendas in ten departments and only withdrew after the government threatened force. The landholders sometimes struck back, as in Olancho, where, aided by the local military commandant, they attacked a UNC training center and killed five peasant leaders.[7] Two foreign priests, one from the United States and the other Canadian, were murdered for trying to aid in the land reform struggle; but, again, unlike the situation in El Salvador, the governement did not condone the murder of priests.

In the midst of the efforts to enforce the agrarian reform act, there was a major political crisis, which by some sort of supposed analogy to the Watergate scandal in the United States, has become known as the Bananagate scandal. In February of 1974, the presidents of Honduras and Panama had met to discuss means of getting a larger revenue from the exportation of bananas. They decided to call a general meeting of Central American states and other exporters, which convened in Panama on 8 March. Represented were Colombia, Ecuador, Costa Rica, Nicaragua, Honduras, Guatemala, and Panama. These formed the Unión de Paises Exportadores de Banano, an organization committed to putting high imposts on the export of the fruit. In Honduras this translated into a fifty-cents-a-crate charge on bananas, which was instituted on 25 April 1974. This new tax was opposed by both Standard Fruit and United Brands (the former UFCO), and the method of levying it drew a protest from the United States ambassador. The ambassador was apparently referring to the suddenness with which the levy was made. But in other quarters the new tax was popular —with the unions, in particular SUTRASFCO, under Napoleón Acevedo Granados, backing the policy of the government.

United Brands was hit harder than was Standard Fruit because it lacked diversification, and the giant firm made a number of protests to the government. Surprisingly enough, these protests turned out to be successful, and on 24 August 1974 the government did an about-face and canceled the tax. Behind the scenes, it was later discovered, the chairman of the board of United Brands, Eli Black, had been bribing Honduran officials. Black, a freewheeling entrepreneur who had taken over United Fruit in a surprise stock raid, had transferred $1,250,000 to the Swiss bank account of Economics Minister Abraham Bennaton Ramos, and had apparently also given sums directly to López Arellano. These facts became known through a United States Senate probe of the activities of multinationals, a probe brought on by the events in Chile. On 3 February 1975 Eli Black threw himself out the window of the twenty-fifth story of his New York headquarters, and shortly afterwards the involvement of the Honduran government with Black became known.[8]

The revelation of Bananagate brought about a military coup in Honduras on 31 March 1975 with Gen. Juan Alberto Mélgar Castro taking control as the chief of state. It was he who had to deal with the agrarian unrest that now gripped the country. Because of the scandal, the focus of this discontent was now the existence of the great banana concessions. The Universidad Nacional Autónoma de Honduras launched a great drive for nationalization in June and was joined by some labor and peasant elements, although the influential Oscar Gale Varela opposed nationalization on the grounds that it would be economically disruptive.[9]

Although the drive for nationalization was unsuccessful, it did succeed in mobilizing peasant forces. The *campesinos'* perception of Mélgar was that he was slowing down the land reform process initated by López Arellano; and so in October the Peasant Front, comprising the major agrarian unions and representing some 150,000 *campesinos,* issued an ultimatum to the new government to implement Decree 170 at once. The chief of state responded by returning to the leadership of the INA the man most identified in the popular mind with land reform, Rigoberto Sandoval Corea.[10] Sandoval, who continued as INA director until March of 1977, made some progress toward fulfilling the terms of the agrarian reform law, but found himself frequently thwarted by other government figures.

One of the country's biggest trouble spots was the commune of Isletas on the north coast. After Hurricane Fifi had ravaged the area, Isletas had been abandoned by Standard Fruit; and a group of *campesinos* had moved in, most of them former banana workers left unemployed after the storm. This seizure was never more than tolerated, although INA did give the peasants some aid. Another source of "help" was the North American Agency AIFLD, despite the frequent charges that in reality both Mélgar Castro and AIFLD were trying to destroy the project by staffing it with tame stooges.[11] These charges led to increasing dissension between the government and the more militant leaders of the commune, and on 12 February 1977 the government invaded Isletas and arrested nine peasant leaders who were charged with misuse of government funds. The National University, through its own unions, became very militant over this issue and aided the jailed peasants.[12] This event led to Sandoval's resignation, and greatly tarnished the reformist image of Mélgar Castro.[13]

In addition to the events at Isletas and the resignation of Sandoval, there was other evidence that the country was moving to the right; for on 4 January 1977 Col. César Elvir Sierra, a friend of reform, was removed as chief of staff of the army. His replacement was Col. Mario Cárcamo Chinchilla, the former defense minister who was replaced in that position by Col. Omar Antonio Zelaya Reyes. Many of the "young turks," or progressives, within the military were shunted aside in an obvious move to make the regime acceptable to conservative interests. On the same day the prolabor minister of labor, Enrique Flores Valeriano, was driven out of office.[14]

Despite these apparently antireform changes in the government, Mélgar still was considered by many as being a progressive military leader. The secretary of the presidency, César Batres, made great strides in returning the country to prosperity. By the middle of 1978, Honduras was prosperous as seldom before in her troubled history. General Mélgar himself was not an unpopular figure. Unlike his counterpart in El Salvador, he liked to portray himself as a man of the people, and was in fact able to circulate freely without armed guards or special fanfare. In the tradition of Carías Andino, he could occasionally be seen strolling down the streets of the capital, just like any ordinary citizen.

There was, however, a virtual moratorium on politics. Perhaps the handsomest building in Tegucigalpa is the National Assembly, but it has stood vacant since 1976, there being in reality no national assembly. Elections were promised for the Assembly, which in turn would elect a president; but such elections kept being put off, first to 1979, and then for still another year. It was officially stated that the reasons for the postponements concerned the lack of electoral machinery for the registration of voters. More likely, the chief of state was waiting until he had consolidated his hold on power, and had ordered his finance minister, Porfirio Zavala Sandoval, who had charge of setting up the process, to deliberately go slow.[15]

The political parties, by now unaccustomed to real contention for power, had grown weak and divided. The once strong Liberals, under the nominal leadership of Modesto Rodas, were split between the faction loyal to former presidential candidate Jorge Buezo Arias and a more left-of-center group led by the rector of UNAH, Carlos Alberto Reina. Ricardo Zúñiga's Nationals likewise were rent by factionalism. The army distrusted both of these traditional political groupings for their factionalism and corruption, and many soldiers would be reluctant to turn power back to the old guard of professional politicos. On the other hand, the most powerful new political force to arise, the Christian Democratic Party, was also distrusted for being radical and, like the PDC in El Salvador, for being linked to the *campesino* union, the UNC, which often contends with the ANACH. These unions did not help the cause of worker solidarity with their own constant bickerings. Their suspicions and divisions have played into the hands of those who wished to maintain military control of the country. The average Honduran takes none of this too seriously. He feels just as free under the soldiers as he felt under the civilians, and he is probably right. More than a century of mostly misgovernment has given the man on the street a very cynical attitude toward both conservatives and reformers.

Indeed, the atmosphere in Honduras at the close of the decade did not appear to be one of repression, elections or no elections. The squads of police and soldiers that prowl the streets and roads of El Salvador were nowhere to be seen. The four major papers of the country, two Liberal and two National in leaning, expressed themselves freely, and the UNAH was regarded as the freest national university in Central America outside of Costa Rica. Labor gave at least qualified support to the Mélgar regime and to Labor Minister Adalberto Discua, the law partner of César Batres. Only the quarrel with El Salvador seemed likely to fire political partisanship. In March 1978 Víctor

Artiles of the CTH attacked the idea of ever letting the Salvadoreans return and compete with native labor. In mid-April the government of Mélgar Castro canceled all permits for travel to El Salvador and subsequent reentry into Honduras. Whatever the government claimed, it appeared that the real reason for this was the fact that many Hondurans were going to El Salvador for medical treatment, a commentary on the state of health care in Honduras. *El Tiempo* of San Pedro Sula (25 April 1978) noted the paradox of the government "trying to achieve final peace with El Salvador and on the other hand completely contradicting itself by prohibiting any kind of relations with the people on the other side of the Goascarán River." Probably the interdiction of the border was designed to be temporary and tactical. Nothing in either domestic or foreign policy indicated that the government of Mélgar Castro was in any real trouble.

Nevertheless, on the evening of 7 August 1978, this government was overthrown in a bloodless coup. The person most responsible for this was General Policarpo Paz García, commander in chief of the armed forces. His principal coconspirators were Air Force Commander Lieutenant Colonel Domingo Alvarez and Police Commander Lt. Col. Amílcar Zelaya Rodríguez. Many saw in this latest coup the hand of Oswaldo López Arellano, who had again managed to be, at least officially, out of the country at the time. César Elvir Sierra, the former chief of staff deposed by Mélgar Castro, was believed to have provided the link between Paz García and the former strong man. It was also believed that members of the National Party were involved in this action; for three seats in the new cabinet formerly under General Paz García went to members of that party, and Ricardo Zúñiga, the former chief minister of López Arellano, was now the unofficial adviser to the chief of state. Further, it was observed that one of the principal conspirators, Colonel Zelaya, was of an old National Party family.[16] In all, the new government looked more conservative than its predecessor. It had, at least by December 1978, still not accorded juridical status to the Christian Democrats, an indispensable condition for that potent new political force to play a role in any new elections. It had further begun to slow still more the promised land reform, bringing complaints from UNC leader Víctor Inocencio Peralta, who declared in October that only 15 per cent of the promised six hundred thousand hectares had been distributed.

The new government further appeared likely to complicate the attempts to arrive at peace with El Salvador. César Batres, the secretary of the presidency, had been immediately replaced for his temerity in calling the change of government a coup. In his place came Gustavo Acosta Mejía, widely regarded as an enemy of El Salvador and a hard-liner on the negotiations. No one in the diplomatic service on the other side of the border appeared to welcome the change. Further, Col. Roberto Palma Gálvez, the foreign minister, resigned in July 1979, declaring that his government had not supported his peace efforts and had put him in a ridiculous position before the OAS.

Despite the political upheavals of the decade, Honduras seemed to have lurched forward toward economic and social progress, while El Salvador had definitely retrogressed. There is even the continued prospect of a return to civilian rule and the possibility of reasonably honest elections in 1980. If some sort of political continuity could be achieved, the future might be fairly bright in this country, traditionally regarded as one of the poorest and most backward of Latin American states.

Chapter 11
Conclusions

When the investigator shines his probing light upon the causality of the war of 1969, he finds this causality to be as multifaceted as a diamond. No single explanation suffices, but that is of course true of all historic events. Nevertheless, weight can be assigned to the various factors that led to the clash.

Remotely, the war has its origin in the original breakup of Central America after independence. This break resulted in the creation of five rival nationalisms, carefully fostered by politicos and militarists for their own aggrandizement. Over the years these nationalisms have become automatic responses in the unsophisticated popular mind. Not only is a *catracho* supposed to hate a *guanaco,* and vice versa but this antagonism extends to every rival national group in the area. Despite the existence of these rival nationalisms there has always existed a drive for unity, which has in turn inevitably reinforced the passion for national exclusiveness. It might be asked how real can the feelings of nationality be in an area which shares a common language, a common religion, common customs, and with the exception of Costa Rica, a common ethnic heritage—for these are the traditional marks of a nation. But the historical factor in nationalism cannot be overlooked. Sometimes the feeling of historical unity can transcend the boundaries of diverse languages, religions, and customs, as in the case of Switzerland, which became a nation through opposition to common foes. In the case of the Central American states, the history has been one of mutual antagonism and frequent war, of which the war of 1969 is simply another example. These national antipathies cannot be given too great a weight in the causes of the 1969 war, for hostile nations sometimes live side by side for centuries without resort to force, but the hostility must be kept in mind. It would also be

167

erroneous to conclude that all Salvadoreans hate Hondurans or the reverse. These are warm and generous peoples who, when not aroused, are more than likely to express their love for their fellow Central Americans in sentimental terms. But it would not be wise to bet one's life on that sentiment carrying over to the next day, however real it might seem at the moment.

A factor which must be assigned considerable weight was the migration of Salvadoreans into Honduras. This migration began early in the century before population pressures in El Salvador became extreme, although it is certainly true that as the desperation of the Salvadorean peasants increased, an additional motive was given to emigrate. Initially, however, it was the pull of Honduras and not the push of population that drove the Salvadoreans across the border.

The presence of some three hundred thousand Salvadoreans represented both a problem and an opportunity when the government of López Arellano decided to implement the land reform laws. On one hand, the Salvadoreans were a complicating factor, a vocal and aggressive force which, as William Durham points out, often aided the Honduran peasants in standing up for their rights.[1] The Salvadoreans also competed for the land that might go to the rural poor, and therein lay the opportunity. If the government could accomplish its land reform without touching the property of the rich and powerful, so much the better. If one could please the peasantry and FENAGH too, with the only casualties being the foreigners, the political circle would be squared, and López Arellano could count on years of office and spoils. To what extent the Sandoval policy of expropriating the untitled lands of the immigrants was a genuinely popular one remains an interesting question. Durham, taking only one small border village as his sample, concludes that there was no real hostility, but my own experiences lead me to believe that the always latent hostility to outsiders had been successfully stirred up by the Honduran press to the point at which the grossest outrages paraded as patriotism.

The question of the frontier was certainly a lesser causal factor in the war than the question of migration and expulsion, but it has nonetheless been a smoldering source of discord for more than a century. Honduras, in particular, has had a long history of border disputes and contentions which have, at times, erupted into violence. While Salvadorean statesmen tend to dismiss the border issue as a red herring designed simply to stall negotiations, and therefore to stall economic and political integration in Central America, their counterparts at the *cancillería* in Tegucigalpa maintain, with some sincerity, that this is an issue which must be settled to bring peace.[2] They can point out, in backing up their claims, that the whole Martínez Argueta affair arose precisely because of the lack of clear frontiers; and this incident, along with the subsequent border penetration of the Sleeping Beauties, sent the two countries down the road to war. In the absence of other severe problems, it is doubtful that the lack of defined frontiers would have led to war; but once the process of hostility had begun, the fluidity of the boundaries made incursions easy and kept tempers rising. Given the war and the current diplomatic climate between the two states, it would certainly seem wise to settle the boundary question for once and all, but the Honduran demand that this be done simultaneously with all other conflict resolutions seems very much like a stall.

Most importantly, the internal situation of each country must also be taken into account in assessing the causes of the war. In El Salvador since the thirties, the noose had been tightening around the necks of the peasantry. There had been an encroachment of the cash-crop haciendas and *fincas* upon the peasant subsistence farms, and this was taking place at a time when there were more and more mouths to feed. Migration out of the country was a convenient safety valve for this pressure upon the land. Both the politicos and the oligarchs welcomed the exodus to Honduras, and feared to see it cut off. On the other hand, these pressures did not appear in 1969 to have reached the critical stage. There was no FECCAS and no UTC in those days, so that the peasants were weak, disorganized, and terrified by memories of 1932. There was still the hope that the PCN promise of land reform might be fulfilled or that an election might substitute some other party, the PDC perhaps, which would institute the necessary changes.

Thus, as far as land reform was concerned, Sánchez Hernández in El Salvador was still dealing with a subcritical mass. His real fear of an explosion had political rather than social causes. Two preceding military regimes had been successively overturned by ambitious younger officers, and Sánchez Hernández knew that he was on trial for his life before his own officer corps. The humiliating arrest of the Sleeping Beauties and the necessity of freeing Martínez Argueta had cost him dearly in prestige before his fellow officers. He could not afford to back down again or to seem weak or vacillating in the face of a crisis. Further, himself a man who was *muy macho*, he could hardly have sat still while he felt his country was being dishonored. The massive expulsions of May and June provided just the kind of crisis to which he must respond, and if the response were successful, it would greatly enhance his chances of peacefully turning over the government to some PCN successor. Popular sentiment, goaded by the oligarchy's newspapers, had begun to heat up with the arrest of Martínez Argueta, and by June of 1969 was in a highly unstable condition which, if no action were taken, might have been ready to back a military coup. At this point his closest military associates must also have been urging the president to action.

In Honduras the López Arellano regime was caught between the pressures of the unions and those of the traditional powers. Land reform had been instituted to pacify the agricultural unions, and the method of carrying it out had been chosen to mollify the oligarchy as well; but these decisions carried the calculated risk of a real explosion with El Salvador, whose military power far exceeded that of Honduras. Even if it did come to a military conflict, the government of Honduras might have reasoned, the OAS would soon stop it, and nothing would unite the hostile elements in Honduras like a war. In actuality the prestige of López Arellano appears to have been somewhat damaged by the war.

Before examining the war, there remains one interesting question which, while not directly related to the origins of the war, still always seems to arise in connection with it. It concerns a very emotionally charged issue for Salvadoreans and for Central Americans in general. The question is whether El Salvador is in fact overpopulated in absolute terms or whether this overpopulation is in fact mythical. If the latter is the case, the blame must lie with the wicked oligarchs and their military henchmen, who have so distributed the land as to freeze out the small farmer. In this supposition all that is necessary to end the so-called overpopulation is a redistribution of the land and a deemphasis of cash crops in favor of food staples. This view was raised by Marco Virgilio Carías in 1971. If, however, the contention is true that El Salvador is absolutely overpopulated, it would suggest that radical measures must be taken to reduce the population. These would have to include some means of family planning. This view is gaining some acceptability in enlightened circles, although it is totally contrary to the entire culture and to the religion of El Salvador. Family planning runs into opposition not only from the clergy but from the entire spectrum of Salvadorean political factions, all of which see it as a Yankee imperialist plot to cut the number of Latin Americans.

The problem really lies with the Malthusian-sounding idea of "absolute overpopulation." Many thoughtful Salvadoreans claim that their country is not overpopulated, for other societies with far more than 570 persons per square mile do quite well. Carías and later Durham, in his careful study, seem to agree. Often the example of Holland is pointed to, a country with a population density of over a thousand persons per square mile that manages to skate along quite nicely. Such contentions overlook certain basic facts. First of all, the population of such industrial countries as Holland is stable. These countries do not have to contend with the problem of having every other person fourteen or younger. The more mature populations of such industrialized states provide a large pool of labor in proportion to the population as a whole. Further, the economies of such countries as Holland or Japan are based upon an infrastructure of highly technical education and a tradition of learning that is centuries old. El Salvador must deal with a population still half illiterate. Neither the government nor the society as a whole appears to have yet perceived that education is itself a natural resource of great importance, and even if a crash program were to be launched tomorrow to achieve such an education base, the results might not bear fruit for half a century. Countries with a high population and without great natural resources can achieve apparent miracles, but when the miracles are examined more closely, they are solidly based upon the conscious choices and extended histories of those countries.

El Salvador will be likely to remain a predominantly agricultural country for the foreseeable future and will not become another Holland. But could it be that, given the agricultural basis, a drastic redistribution of the wealth in land might solve the pressures of population? There are several observations which could be made here. First of all, those who have the land show scant indication of being willing to relinquish it gracefully. It will probably have to be torn from their grasp in an upheaval dwarfing that of 1932. The new junta may achieve such a miracle, but miracles are by definition highly improbable events.

Barring great strides in land reform, El Salvador will have to continue within in the context of current landholding patterns, and in such a context there are indeed too many people. Even if the unlikely took place, it is hard to see that a diminution of export crops in favor of food crops would really solve the problems of the country. El Salvador, which produces so little of its nonagricultural needs, must export or perish as a modern society. Again, given an export economy, there are too many Salvadoreans for the land. This may not be absolute overpopulation, but it is close enough for all practical purposes.

To turn to the war itself, the vexatious question remains as to what was intended by the Salvadorean military operations of July 1969. If documents exist that clearly indicate the intent of the Salvadorean military, my investigation has not been able to uncover them. Only the statements of the principal participants are on record, and these, as we have seen, are contradictory. It is my belief that, having decided to roll the iron dice, the military was willing to go where the roll indicated. The plan was laid, in frank imitation of Israel, for a massive enveloping surprise attack; but should it bog down, as it did, they could always contend that they had envisioned no more than a chastisement along the border, similar to the Chinese chastisement of Vietnam in 1979. If the drive lived up to their hopes, they might have toppled López Arellano and vindicated themselves for the humiliation of the Martínez Argueta fiasco. It did not live up to their expectations, and eventually the troops had to be withdrawn, though not from all the territory which Honduras claims.

The war may well not have been nearly as sanguinary as the original inflammatory claims of both sides suggested, but in terms of the disruption of human life, the cost was high. In a corner of the world where so many lead lives on the margin of extinction, any disruption can be fatal in terms of lost food production, physical exhaustion, and the break with local patterns of mutual help and interaction. In this sense the war cost more than either side could afford. The hundreds of thousands of dispossessed were the real casualties of the war.

A question which arises frequently in regard to the war of 1969 is that of the role of the United States. There is a tendency in Central America to blame everything except Hurricane Fifi on the North Americans. This is what I call "the colossus-of-the-North syndrome." Given the role of the United States in Guatemala, the Dominican Republic and Chile, this fear is hardly without justification; but there is no evidence that the United States government followed a coherent policy during the war of support for either side. The chief efforts of North American diplomats appear to have been directed at cooling the whole situation.

The result of the war for El Salvador has been a decade of unparalleled civil strife, to which there is no end in sight. This is because the war not only injured the economy but also turned the country in upon itself. Those problems which had not reached the critical stage before, those problems of population and subsistence which could be hidden and disguised before, now burst into the open. The disillusioning experience of 1972 destroyed all real hope of peaceful political change within the foreseeable future. The result was the resort to terrorism, always the weapon of those driven mad with desperation. Terrorism is never something to be condoned; but if a government seals off all other avenues of effecting desperately needed changes, given the temper of the modern world, terrorism is an almost certain result.

The need for change in El Salvador goes far beyond any repartition of the land, though that might be a step in the right direction. The whole framework of ideas about the nature and purpose of society would have to be transformed to create a society based on mutual sharing of the increasingly scarce resources of that beautiful, but stricken, land. The country is headed toward eventual disaster unless the energetic and far-sighted efforts of Salvadoreans save her.

For Honduras the war created a series of ironies. At first the economy faltered, but this led to redoubled efforts to find new sources of imports and new products to export. By the end of the decade, the country had made some real progress. The Salvadoreans had invaded to cripple Honduras if she would not change her policies; they ended by benefiting her. There is irony too in the fact that despite the highly touted claims that the Common Market would help every country in the area, Honduras found her salvation in breaking with the MCCA.

López Arellano appeared at first discredited by the war. The country was turned over to a Nationalist president. But that president neglected the land reform which the exodus of the Salvadoreans should have facilitated, and the result was that López Arellano again seized power, the beneficiary of governmental inaction. And yet he could not hold it. The very efforts his government made to increase their revenue from banana exports tempted the officials of that government beyond their resistance, and they found in Eli Black someone who would not scruple to use their venality. The resulting scandal toppled the government, but it has not brought political stability. Two coups later, Honduras is still looking for a return to normal political life. The political instability, verging at times on anarchy in many departments, has hindered the drive for land reform; but under López Arellano and Mélgar Castro some land has been distributed, and the peasant has become much more politically effective than his Salvadorean counterpart.

In the short run El Salvador suffered and Honduras benefited from the breakup of the MCCA, but in the long run some return to the ideas of the Common Market appears to be necessary. Jeffery Nugent, in his study, pointed out that the benefits of the formation of the Common Market in Central America may have been quite substantial.[3] Eventually, Central Americans are going to have to sit down around a conference table and try to glue this commercial union back together again. The war of 1969 has unfortunately made this task much more difficult than it was originally.

Political unity seems even more remote. As of now, five different sets of political leaders, ranging from the democratically elected president of Costa Rica through the revolutionary junta of Nicaragua and El Salvador to the conservative, military-backed regimes of Honduras and Guatemala, enjoy the fruits of Central American office holding. It seems highly unrealistic to imagine the political masters of any of these countries altruistically submerging themselves in a larger unit. Only some loose federation, such as has been achieved before, appears even a distant possibility. The drive to unification is there, but the counterforces are much greater. Almost every Central American assures one that the unification must come some day, but that day is always indefinitely postponed. The war of 1969 postponed it still further, and it may never come; but then, as the saying goes, "never is a long time." In the meantime people continue to live in hovels and to wonder what peculiar stroke of fate put them in the front line of a war they little understood.

Postscript: On October 30, 1980, a treaty of peace between El Salvador and Honduras was signed in Lima, Peru, by Foreign Ministers Fidel Chávez Mena and César Elvir Sierra. The territorial settlement and many other issues remained under negotiation.

Notes

CHAPTER 1

1. Eddy E. Jiménez, *La Guerra No Fue de Fútbol*, p. 113. The figures are his except for the killed and wounded, which he estimates at half again as great. Juan Ramón Ardón, *Días de Infamia*, pp. 198–205, estimates, on the other hand, that only ninety-nine Hondurans were killed and sixty-six wounded, a figure which seems ridiculously low. For further estimates see chap. 7.

2. See Thomas P. Anderson, "The Great Fútbol War," pp. 479–80; and Larry L. Pippin, "Soccer War or Demographic Conflict?", pp. 15–21.

3. Government of Honduras, Oficina Central de Información de SECTIN, *El Conflicto de un Siglo*, pp. 9–11.

4. Thomas L. Karnes, *The Failure of Union*, p. 68.

5. Ibid., pp. 70–83.

6. Ibid., pp. 86–88.

7. Mario Rodríguez, *Central America*, p. 92.

8. Charles David Kepner, Jr., *Social Aspects of the Banana Industry*, pp. 30–31.

9. William S. Stokes, *Honduras*, p. 39. Karnes, *Failure of Union*, pp. 127–28.

10. Karnes, *Failure of Union*, pp. 162–63.

11. Franklin D. Parker, *The Central American Republics*, p. 81.

12. Karnes, *Failure of Union*, p. 166.

13. Ibid., p. 172.

14. Parker, *Central American Republics*, p. 81.

15. Karnes, *Failure of Union*, p. 190.

16. Stokes, *Honduras*, p. 52.

17. Jiménez, *La Guerra*, pp. 42–45. Costa Rica ratified in 1963.

CHAPTER 2

1. David Browning, *El Salvador*, p. 5.

2. David R. Reynolds, *Rapid Development in Small Economies*, p. 11.

3. Browning, *El Salvador*, pp. 71–73.

4. Ibid., p. 135.

5. Ibid., pp. 141–144.

6. Everett A. Wilson, "The Crisis of National Integration in El Salvador," p. 34.

7. Wilson, "Crisis," pp. 44, 132, 285. Browning, *El Salvador*, pp. 149, 159. William H. Durham, *Scarcity and Survival in Central America*, p. 36.

8. Reynolds, *Rapid Development*, p. 14.

9. Abel Cuenca, *El Salvador*, p. 17. Durham, *Scarcity and Survival*, p. 36.

10. Browning, *El Salvador*, p. 88.

11. Alastair White, *El Salvador*, p. 87.

12. Marco Virgilio Carías et al., *La Guerra Inutil*, p. 15.

13. Jorge Schlesinger, *Revolución Comunista*, (Guatemala City: N.P., 1946), pp. 16–17.

14. White, *El Salvador*, p. 118.

15. Thomas P. Anderson, *Matanza*, p. 154.

16. Wilson, "Crisis," pp. 59, 132.

17. Richard N. Adams, *Cultural Surveys of Panama, Nicaragua, Guatemala, El Salvador and Honduras*, pp. 462–63.

18. Alejandro Dagoberto Maroquín, the noted Salvadorean sociologist, estimated 80 per cent in an unpublished manuscript.

19. Anderson, *Matanza*, p. 12.

20. Wilson, "Crisis," p. 187.

21. Ibid., pp. 24, 114–15.

22. These facts and what follows about the revolt of 1932 are from Anderson, *Matanza*.

23. The life of Miguel Marmol is well told in a book by the late Salvadorean poet Roque Dalton, *Miguel Marmol*.

24. White, *El Salvador*, p. 91. He suggests that the "idealist-liberal" leader Prudencio Alfaro was behind it.

25. Anderson, *Matanza*, p. 136.

26. Osborne, Lilly de Jongh, *Four Keys to El Salvador*, p. 184.

27. White, *El Salvador*, p. 104.

28. Ibid., p. 105.

29. Franklin D. Parker, *The Central American Republics*, pp. 156–57.

30. Reynolds, *Rapid Development*, pp. 19–20.

31. Durham, *Scarcity and Survival*, pp. 30–33.

32. Browning, *El Salvador*, p. 240. J. Mayone Stycos and Cornell Capa, *Margin of Life*, p. 24.

33. Browning, *El Salvador*, p. 268.

34. *This Week: Central America and Panama*, 4 September, 1978. Stycos and Capa, *Margin of Life*, p. 14.

35. Eddy Jiménez, *La Guerra No Fue de Fútbol*, p. 28. Carías et al., *La Guerra Inutil*, pp. 254–55.

36. White, *El Salvador*, p. 123.

37. Browning, *El Salvador*, p. 262. He comments: "If a small area of good land is left vacant and unguarded anywhere in El Salvador, it is certain to be covered with huts and cultivated plots in a very short time."

38. Stycos and Capa, *Margin of Life*, p. 68.

39. Ibid., pp. 24–27. Durham, *Scarcity and Survival*, chap. 11.

40. Durham, *Scarcity and Survival*, chap. 3.

41. White, *El Salvador*, pp. 144–48.

42. Ibid., pp. 147–48.

43. Stycos and Capa, *Margin of Life*, p. 13.

CHAPTER 3

1. William S. Stokes, *Honduras*, pp. 31–33.

2. Franklin D. Parker, *The Central American Republics*, p. 186.

3. Ibid.

4. Benjamín Villanueva, "The Role of Institutional Innovations in the Economic Development of Honduras," p. 6.

5. Parker, *Central American Republics*, pp. 196–99.

6. Dr. Jorge Fidel Durón, lawyer and historian, is a member of the mixed commission on boundaries and peace.

7. Government of Honduras, Oficina Central de Información de SECTIN, *El Conflicto de un Siglo*, pp. 15–17.

8. *Exposición del Excelentísimo Dr. Francisco José Guerrero, Ministro de Relaciones Exteriores de El Salvador en la Sexta Sesión Plenaria Celebrada el Seis de Octubre de 1969*, given at the OAS, in the archives of the Ministerio de Relaciones Exteriores de El Salvador.

9. Stokes, *Honduras*, pp. 44–45, 209–16.

10. Ibid., pp. 220–24.

11. Charles David Kepner, Jr., *Social Aspects of the Banana Industry*, pp. 34–41.

12. Stacy May and Galo Plaza Lasso, *The United Fruit Company in Latin America*, p. 10.

13. Kepner, *Banana Industry*, pp. 73–74. Villanueva, "Institutional Innovations," p. 7.

14. May and Plaza Lasso, *United Fruit Company*, p. 16.

15. Kepner, *Banana Industry*, pp. 53–54, 76.

16. Ibid., pp. 53–55, 67.

17. May and Plaza Lasso, *United Fruit Company*, pp. 79, 86, 152, 158.

18. Eddy E. Jiménez, *La Guerra No Fue de Fútbol*, p. 24.

19. Villanueva, "Institutional Innovations," p. 7.

20. José Luis González Sibrián, *Las Cien Horas*, p. 12.

21. Thomas P. McCann, *An American Company*, p. 40.

22. Rafael Leiva Vivas, *Honduras*, p. 23.

23. Kepner, *Banana Industry*, pp. 124–25, 172.

24. Stokes, *Honduras,* p. 191.
25. Ibid., p. 237.
26. Parker, *Central American Republics,* p. 188.
27. John D. Martz, *Central America,* pp. 114–16.
28. Ibid., p. 122. Stokes, *Honduras,* pp. 56–57.
29. Martz, *Central America,* pp. 126–27. Villanueva, "Institutional Innovations," p. 27.

CHAPTER 4

1. Marco Virgilio Carías et al., *La Guerra Inutil,* pp. 34–35. Rafael Leiva Vivas, *Honduras,* p. 41. Benjamín Villanueva, "The Role of Institutional Innovations in the Economic Development of Honduras," p. 19.
2. Villanueva, "Institutional Innovations," pp. 14, 19. However, Paul Vinelli, president of Banco Atlántida, in an interview pointed out that there was no great concentration of wealth in a few hands as in El Salvador.
3. William H. Durham, *Scarcity and Survival, in Central America,* chap. 4.
4. Charles David Kepner, Jr., *Social Aspects of the Banana Industry,* pp. 182–83, 188, 199.
5. John D. Martz, *Central America,* p. 131.
6. Ibid., pp. 131–40.
7. Rafael Leiva Vivas, *Un País en Honduras,* p. 89.
8. Martz, *Central America,* pp. 147–48.
9. Ibid., p. 159. Franklin D. Parker, *The Central American Republics,* p. 192.
10. Gary W. Wynia, *Politics and Planners,* p. 17.
11. Government of El Salvador, Ministerio de Relaciones Exteriores de El Salvador, *El Salvador y su Diferendo con Honduras,* p. 46.
12. Eddy E. Jiménez, *La Guerra No Fue de Fútbol,* p. 90.
13. Villanueva, "Institutional Innovations," p. 29.
14. Leiva Vivas, *Un País,* p. 12.
15. Jiménez, *La Guerra,* p. 91.
16. Leiva Vivas, *Un País,* p. 11.
17. Ibid., pp. 60–63.
18. Ibid., pp. 8–9.
19. Roberto Perdomo Paredes (ambassador of Honduras to OAS), "Nota de 30 de Septiembre de 1969 al Presidente Interimo de la 10a. Reunión de Ministros de Relaciones Exteriores," in the archives of the Ministerio de Relaciones Exteriores de Honduras. J. Mayone Stycos and Cornell Capa, *Margin of Life,* pp. 9, 115–16. Stycos and Capa (*Margin of Life,* p. 71) record a laborer of this time earning twenty-five cents (in U.S. money) a day plus a meal, except during the cotton harvest, when he got $1.50 a day. And this was in 1969!
20. Jiménez, *La Guerra,* p. 92.

21. Carías et al., *La Guerra Inutil*, pp. 128–132.
22. Leiva Vivas, *Un País*, p. 41.
23. Jiménez, *La Guerra*, p. 49.
24. Stycos and Capa, *Margin of Life*, p. 49.
25. Jiménez, *La Guerra*, p. 49.
26. Ibid., p. 21.
27. Ibid., p. 22.
28. Secretario Permanente del Tratado General de Integración Económica Centroamericana, *El Desarrollo Integrado de CentroAmerica en la Presente Década*, p. 10. Jeffery B. Nugent, *Economic Integration in Central America*, p. 75.
29. Secretario Permanente, *El Desarrollo*, p. 13.
30. Nugent, *Economic Integration*, p. 10.
31. Secretario Permanente, *El Desarrollo*, p. 17.
32. Leiva Vivas, *Un País*, p. 41.
33. Wynia, *Politics and Planners*, p. 115.
34. Leiva Vivas, *Un País*, p. 29.
35. Ibid., p. 15.
36. Ibid., p. 34.
37. José Luis González Sibrián, *Las Cien Horas*, p. 20.

CHAPTER 5

1. José Luis González Sibrián, *Las Cien Horas*, p. 30.
2. Charles David Kepner, Jr., *Social Apsects of the Banana Industry*, pp. 173–74.
3. Luis Gallegos Valdes, *Diario de Hoy* (San Salvador), 16 June 1967.
4. *Patria* (San Salvador), 13 and 17 July 1929, quoted in Everett A. Wilson, "The Crisis of National Integration in El Salvador," p. 129.
5. Ibid. H. Roberto Herrera Cáceres, *El Diferendo Hondureño-Salvadoreño*, p. 15.
6. Marco Virgilio Carías et al., *La Guerra Inutil*, pp. 62–63.
7. Eddy E. Jiménez, *La Guerra No Fue de Fútbol*, pp. 82–84.
8. Informe de don Jacinto Pohl h., 16 October 1979, in the archives of the Ministerio de Relaciones Exteriores de El Salvador. Carías et al., *La Guerra Inutil*, p. 44.
9. Jiménez, *La Guerra*, pp. 83–87, quoting a report in *Estudios Centroamericanos* of July 1969.
10. J. Mayone Stycos and Cornell Capa, *Margin of Life*, p. 44.
11. Informe.
12. Ibid.
13. Government of El Salvador, Ministerio de Relaciones Exteriores, *El Salvador y su Diferendo con Honduras*, pp. 49–50.
14. Ibid., p. 52.
15. González Sibrián, *Las Cien Horas*, pp. 32, 35–36.

16. Ms. Jaime Chacón P., in the archives of the Ministerio de Relaciones Exteriores de El Salvador.

17. *El Pueblo* (Tegucigalpa), 24 December 1966.

18. Juan Ramón Ardón, *Días de Infamia*, p. 115.

19. Comment of Virgilio Gálvez Madrid, a former member of the Honduran boundary commission, and the last Honduran ambassador to El Salvador.

20. *Juicio Penal*, no. 188, 1966, in the archives of the Ministerio de Relaciones Exteriores de El Salvador.

21. There is a memorandum to this effect by the then Chancellor Tiburcio Carías Castillo, "Origen de los Conflictos Fronterizos entre Honduras y El Salvador," bound in the unedited collection of documents "Expediente Confidencial sobre Incidente Ocurido el 25 de Mayo de 1967 en la Hacienda de 'Dolores'," in the archives of the Ministerio de Relaciones Exteriores de El Salvador.

22. Carías et al., *La Guerra Inutil*, pp. 73–74.

23. There is some discrepancy in the actual numbers involved. *La Prensa Gráfica* (San Salvador), 29 June 1967, lists thirty-nine soldiers by name and two officers; but a secret note from Lopez Arellano to his chief of special security, Major José Antonio Pérez l. speaks of forty-seven prisoners, that is, forty-one soldiers, two officers, and four civilian drivers. The *Informe de Labores del Poder Ejecutivo en El Ramo de Relaciones Exteriores* (Government of El Salvador, Ministerio de Relaciones Exteriores, p. 62) speaks of forty-one soldiers and two officers being returned.

24. Dispatch of 6 June 1967, 12:35 P.M., in files of Ministerio de Relaciones Exteriores de Honduras.

25. José René Barón Ferrufino, *Penetración Comunista en El Salvador*, pp. 112–18.

26. Juan Ramón Ardón, *Días de Infamia*, p. 116.

27. For understandable reasons the official shall be nameless. General José Alberto Medrano also agrees with the basic theory.

28. *El Pueblo*, 24 June 1968, gives an account of the whole story.

29. Government of El Salvador, *El Salvador y su Diferendo*, p. 61.

30. Document in "Expediente Confidencial."

31. *New York Times*, 12 March 1968.

32. *Miami Herald*, 7 June 1968.

33. Government of El Salvador, *Informe de Labores*, p. 62.

34. According to *El Cronista*, 22 July 1968, even the arms were returned.

CHAPTER 6

1. José René Barón Ferrufino, *Penetración Comunista en El Salvador*, p. 129.

2. J. Mayone Stycos and Cornell Capa, *Margin of Life*, pp. 122–23, 128–29.

Notes (pp. 92–108)

3. José Luis González Sibrián, *Las Cien Horas*, p. 43.
4. In the files of the Ministerio de Relaciones Exteriores de El Salvador.
5. Government of El Salvador, Ministerio de Relaciones Exteriores, *Informe de Labores del Poder Ejecutivo en El Ramo de Relaciones Exteriores*, pp. 64–65.
6. Joseph E. Maleady, *Background El Salvador—Honduras Conflict* (San Salvador: n.p., 1969), p. 2.
7. Tiburcio Carías Castillo to Francisco José Guerrero, 19 June 1969, "Correspondencia Despachado de Mayo-Junio, 1969," in the files of the Ministerio de Relaciones Exteriores de Honduras.
8. Ibid. Carta de 25 de Junio.
9. Comisión Interamericana de Derechos Humanos, *Informe Preliminar de la Comisión* (Washington, D.C.: Organization of American States, 1969), p. 13.
10. Ibid.
11. The speaker referred to may be Modesto Rodas Alvarado.
12. Horacio Mélgar Pinto to Francisco José Guerrero, 2 de Julio de 1969, "Correspondencia General Recibida," in the files of the Ministerio de Relaciones Exteriores de El Salvador.
13. In "Documentos y Varios Fotocopias," an unedited collection in the archives of the Ministerio de Relaciones Exteriores de Honduras.
14. "Copias de Declaraciones Autenticadas Vendidas por los Expulsados de la Republica de Honduras," in the files of the Ministerio de Relaciones Exteriores de El Salvador, nos. 1, 4, and 8. See also Government of El Salvador, Ministerio de Relaciones Exteriores, *El Salvador y su Diferendo con Honduras*, pp. 194–97.
15. Franciso Dheming to Francisco José Guerrero, 30 June 1969, in "Correspondencia General Recibida."
16. *Informe Preliminar*, pp. 14–15.
17. As stated in *La Prensa Gráfica*, 27 June 1969.
18. Tiburcio Carías Castillo to Galo Plaza Lasso, 8 July 1969, in "Correspondencia Despachadó," Julio 1969.
19. *Informe Preliminar*, pp. 14–15.
20. Francisco José Guerrero to Tiburcio Carías Castillo, 19 June 1969, in the archives of the Ministerio de Relaciones Exteriores de El Salvador.
21. Francisco José Guerrero to Tiburcio Carías Castillo, 26 June 1969.
22. The transcript of the broadcast is in the archives of the Ministerio de Relaciones Exteriores de Honduras.

CHAPTER 7

1. Stephen Webre, *José Napoleón Duarte and the Christian Democratic Party in Salvadoran Politics*, pp. 114–15.
2. Quoted in Eddy E. Jiménez, *La Guerra No Fue de Fútbol*, p. 11.
3. Luis Lovo Castelar, *La Guardia Nacional en Campaña*, p. 39.

4. Tiburcio Carías Castillo to Excelentisimo Señor Carlos Holguin, Embajador de Colombia, Presidente del Consejo de la OEA, 26 July 1969, in the files of the Ministerio de Relaciones Exteriores de Honduras.

5. Government of El Salvador, Ministerio de Relaciones Exteriores, *El Salvador y su Diferendo con Honduras*, p. 117.

6. Tiburcio Carías Castillo to Ricardo Midence, 13 July 1969, in "Documentos y Varios Fotocopias," an unedited collection in the files of the Ministerio de Relaciones Exteriores de El Salvador.

7. As quoted in *El Día* (Honduras), 4 June 1968.

8. Juan Ramón Ardón, *Días de Infamia*, pp. 22, 35, 56, 135.

9. Marco Virgilio Carías et al. *La Guerra Inutil*, pp. 306–8.

10. Lovo Castelar, *La Guardia*, pp. 14–15.

11. José Luis González Sibrián, *Las Cien Horas*, p. 157. Orlando Henríquez, *En el Cielo Escribieron Historia*, pp. 23–24. In addition the Hondurans had seventeen transports and twelve light aircraft.

12. Henríquez, *El Cielo*, pp. 86–89. González Sibrián, *Las Cien Horas*, p. 165.

13. Jiménez, *La Guerra*, p. 113.

14. Asdrúbal Ramírez, *Los Militares Patriotas y La Revolución Hondureña*, pp. 23, 32.

15. González Sibrián, *Las Cien Horas*, p. 172. Lovo Castelar, *La Guardia*, pp. 31–34.

16. This I took down as he spoke. I learned last year that he had been killed some time after the war.

17. Peter Grose, "OAS Peace Move is Backed by U.S.," *New York Times*, 16 July 1969.

18. William Montalbano, "Defiant El Salvador Refuses to Withdraw from Honduras," *Chicago Daily News*, 22 July 1969.

19. Jiménez, *La Guerra*, p. 128.

20. *San Francisco Examiner*, 29 July 1969.

21. William H. Durham, *Scarcity and Survival in Central America*, p. 1.

22. González Sibrián, *Las Cien Horas*, pp. 139–40. Lovo Castelar, *La Guardia*, p. 158.

23. Ardón, *Días de Infamia*, pp. 198–205.

24. *Chicago Tribune*, 27 July 1969.

25. Government of El Salvador, *El Salvador y su Diferendo*, p. 122.

26. See Durham, *Scarcity and Survival*, p. 154, on attitudes towards Salvadoreans in Langue.

27. Grose, "OAS Peace Move."

28. Thomas P. McCann, *An American Company*, pp. 165–68. He is not completely reliable on the war, even managing to get its year wrong: 1970 instead of 1969.

CHAPTER 8

1. Mary Jane Reid Martz, *The Central American Soccer War*, p. 90.

2. Tiburcio Carías Castillo to his delegation, in "Documentos y Varios Fotocopias," an unedited collection in the files of the Ministerio de Relaciones Exteriores de El Salvador.

3. *Acta de la Segunda Sesión Plenaria de OEA* (Washington, D.C.: Organization of American States, 1969), Document 30, 30 July 1969, p. 10.

4. Government of El Salvador, Ministerio de Relaciones Exteriores, *Informe de Labores del Poder Ejecutivo en el Ramo de Relaciones Exteriores, 1968–69,* AX 12–16.

5. *Decimatercera Reunión de Consulta de Ministros de Relaciones de OEA* (Washington, D.C.: Organization of American States, 1969), Document 41, 25 August 1969, p. 10.

6. *Tercer Informe de la Comisión de la Decimatercera Reunión de Consulta de Ministros de Relaciones Exteriores* (Washington, D.C.: Organization of American States, 1969, 4 November 1969.

7. Eddy E. Jiménez, *La Guerra No Fue de Fútbol,* pp. 15, 65.

8. Ibid., pp. 72–75.

9. H. Roberto Herrera Cáceres, *El Diferendo Hondureño-Salvadoreño,* pp. 77, 99.

10. M. J. R. Martz, *Soccer War,* p. 79.

11. "Informe Presentado a la Comisión de la XIII Reunión de Consulta por El Excelentisimo Señor Ministro de Relaciones Exteriores de Honduras," 13 April 1973, in the files of the Ministerio de Relaciones Exteriores de Honduras.

12. "Acta de la Reunión de los Ministros de Relaciones Exteriores de El Salvador y de Honduras, Celebrada Conjuntamente con la Comisión Especial de Organo de Consulta," 13 April 1973, in the files of the Ministerio de Relaciones Exteriores de El Salvador.

13. "Documento que el Gobierno de la Republica de El Salvador Presenta a la Comisión Especial de Organo de Consulta," 13 April 1973, in the files of the Ministerio de Relaciones Exteriores de El Salvador.

14. Herrera Cáceres, *El Diferendo,* p. 32.

15. Government of Honduras, Oficina Central de Información SECTIN, *El Conflicto de un Siglo,* p. 29.

16. Memo in the files of the Ministerio de Relaciones Exteriores de El Salvador.

17. Herrera Cáceres, *El Diferendo,* p. 75.

CHAPTER 9

1. William Durham, *Scarcity and Survival,* p. 59

2. Alastair White, *El Salvador,* p. 228.

3. *Latin America,* 9 August 1974.

4. *New York Times,* 5 and 27 August 1975.

5. Eddy Jiménez, *La Guerra No Fue de Fútbol,* p. 157.

6. Ibid., p. 159. Juan Hernández-Pico and others, *El Salvador 1971–1972,* p. 144.

7. Thomas P. Anderson, "El Salvador," in *Yearbook on International Communist Affairs*, 1975, pp. 511–12; 1976, pp. 478–80; 1977, pp. 448–50; 1978, pp. 376–78.

8. Ibid., 1977, p. 449. *Latin America*, 2 April 1976.

9. Durham, *Scarcity and Survival*, p. 167.

10. *ANEP Memoria, 1976–1977* (San Salvador: Asociación Nacional de La Empresa Privada, 1977), pp. 58–59.

11. Robert Drinan, *Human Rights in El Salvador*, p. 9n.

12. *Latin America*, 28 February 1975.

13. *El Salvador: An Amnesty International USA Campaign Booklet*, October 1978, p. 7.

14. Drinan, *Human Rights*, pp. 55–63.

15. Ibid., p. 68

16. *El Salvador Reports*, May and August 1978.

17. Drinan, *Human Rights*, p. 4.

18. Jiménez, *La Guerra*, p. 65.

19. Durham, *Scarcity and Survival*, p. 167.

CHAPTER 10

1. Eddy E. Jiménez, *La Guerra No Fue de Fútbol*, p. 153.

2. Edmundo Valades, *Los Contratos del Diablo*, pp. 50–52.

3. Marco Virgilo Carías et al., *La Guerra Inutil*, p. 32.

4. Rafael Leiva Vivas, *Un País en Honduras*, p. 146.

5. Interview with Paul Vinelli, president of Banco Atlántida.

6. William H. Durham, *Scarcity and Survival in Central America*, chap. 6.

7. Ibid.

8. Valades, *Los Contratos*, pp. 82, 84, 105–6.

9. Ibid., pp. 127, 146.

10. Durham, *Scarcity and Survival*, chap. 6.

11. *Latin American Political Report*, 28 April 1978.

12. *Match Box* (Amnesty International USA), Spring 1978. *El Pulgarcito* (San Francisco), August 1978.

13. The official version was that Sandoval left because of his poor handling of the Bajo Aguan land-reform project.

14. *Latin American Political Report*, 21 January 1977.

15. Ibid., 21 July 1978.

16. Ibid., 18 August and 1 December 1978.

CHAPTER 11

1. William H. Durham, *Scarcity and Survival in Central America*, chap. 6.

2. At the Central American conference held by the Consejo Superior Universitario Centroamericano, at San José, Costa Rica, 3–7 June 1974, the Honduran ambassador to Costa Rica, Señor Alvaro Puerto, declared that the major cause of the war was the failure to establish definite frontiers.

3. Jeffery B. Nugent, *Economic Integration in Central America*, p. 145.

Bibliography

PRINTED WORKS

Adams, Richard N. *Cultural Surveys of Panama, Nicaragua, Guatemala, El Salvador and Honduras*. Washington, D.C.: Pan-American Sanitary Bureau, 1957.

Alvarado, Néstor Enrique. *El Día que Rugio la Tierra*. Tegucigalpa: n.p., 1969.

Anderson, Charles W. "El Salvador: The Army as Reformer." *Political Systems of Latin America*, Edited by Martin C. Needler. Princeton, N.J.: Van Nostrand, 1964.

Anderson, Thomas P. "The Great Fútbol War." *Commonweal* (8 August 1969): 479–80.

———. *Matanza: El Salvador's Communist Revolt of 1932*. Lincoln: University of Nebraska Press, 1971.

———. "The Social and Cultural Roots of Political Violence in Central America." *Agressive Behavior* (1976): 249–55.

Ardón, Juan Ramón. *Días de Infamia*. Tegucigalpa: Imprenta Calderon, 1970.

Arellano Bonilla, R. *¡Basta! ¡Para los Hondureños Unicamente!* Tegucigalpa: n.p., 1970.

Barón Ferrufino, José René. *Penetración Comunista en El Salvador: Veinte Años de Traición*. San Savador: Editorial Ahora, 1970.

Browning, David. *El Savador: Landscape and Society*. Oxford: Clarendon Press, 1971.

Bustamante Maceo, Gregorio. *Historia Militar de El Salvador*. San Salvador: n.p., 1951.

Cable, Vincent. "The Football War and the Central American Common Market." *International Affairs* 45 (1969): 658–71.

Carías, Marco Virgilio. *Análisis del Conflicto entre Honduras y El Salvador*. Tegucigalpa: Universidad Nacional Autónoma de Honduras, 1969.

Carías, Marco Virgilio, and Slutsky, Daniel, eds. *La Guerra Inutil: Análisis Socio-economico del Conflicto entre Honduras y El Salvador*. San Jose: EDUCA, 1971.

Carr, Archie Fairly. *High Jungles and Low*. Gainesville: University of Florida Press, 1953.

Bibliography

Cline, William R., and Delgado, Enrique, eds. *Economic Integration in Central America*. Washington, D.C.: The Brookings Institution, 1978.

Colindres, Eduardo. *Fundamentos Económicos de la Burguesia Savadoreña*. San Salvador: UCA/Editores, 1977.

———. "La Tenencia de la Tierra en El Salvador." *Estudios Centroamericanos* 31 (1976): 463–72.

Conde Salazar, Pablo. "El Salvador: 1969." *Cuadernos Americanos* 156 (1969): 7–19.

Cruz, Ramón E. *Problemas Territoriales Centroamericanos: Derechos de Honduras*. Tegucigalpa: Sociedad de Geografia e Historia de Honduras, 1967.

Cuenca, Abel. *El Savador: Una Democracia Cafetalera*. Mexico, D.F.: ARR-Centro Editorial, 1962.

Dalton, Roque. *El Salvador*. La Habana: Biblioteca Nacional "José Martí," 1963.

Davson, Cyril. *The Elusive Trail*. Edinburgh and London: William Blackwood and Sons, 1927.

Díaz Chavez, Filander. *Honduras: Condiciones Económicas*. San Salvador: Editorial Universitario, 1965.

———. *Las Raices del Hambre y de la Rebeldiá a la Explotación: Un Ensayo sobre la "Pereza."* Tegucigalpa. Imprenta Calderon, 1962.

Dodd, Thomas J., Jr. "La Guerra de Fútbol en Centroamerica," *Revista Conservadora del Pensamiento Centroamericano* 23 (1970): 30–31.

Domínguez, Raúl Alberto. *Ascenso al Poder y Descenso del General Oswaldo López Arellano*. Tegucigalpa: n.p., 1975.

Drinan, Robert; McAward, John; and Anderson, Thomas P. *Human Rights in El Salvador–1978: Report of the Finding of an Investigatory Mission*. Boston: Unitarian Universalist Service Committee, 1978.

Durham, William H. *Scarcity and Survival in Central America: Ecological Origins of the Soccer War*. Stanford, Calif.: Stanford University Press, 1979.

Durón Jorge Fidel. *La Batalla de Washington*. Tegucigalpa: Imprenta Calderon, 1969.

Fuentes Rivera, Luis. *El Conflicto Honduras–El Salvador: Aspectos Politicos, Sociales y Económicos*. San Salvador: n.p., 1969.

Gerstein, J. A. "Conflicto Honduras-Salvador." *Foro Internacional* 11 (1971): 552–69.

Geyer, Georgie Anne. "From Here to Eternity: How a Priest-Congressman and the President of Georgetown University Have Tried to Stop Murder, but Not Necessarily Revolution, in Tiny El Salvador," *Washington Post Magazine*, 10 September 1978, pp. 8–17.

González Sibrián, José Luis. *Las Cien Horas: La Guerra de Legitima Defensa de la Republica de El Salvador*. San Salvador: Tipografia Offset Central, 1972.

Bibliography

Government of El Salvador, Ministerio de Defensa, Comisión Mixta de Investigación História. *La Barbarie Hondureña y los Derechos Humanos: Proceso de una Agresión*. San Salvador: Ministerio de Defensa, 1969.

———, Ministerio de Justicia. "Juicio Penal de J. A. Martínez Argueta, Fausto López y Santiago López." Case 188, 1961.

———, Ministerio de Ralaciones exteriores. *El Salvador y su Diferendo con Honduras: Nuestra Lucha por los Derechos Humanos*. San Salvador: Imprenta Nacional, 1970.

———, Ministerio de Relaciones Exteriores. *Informes de Labores del Poder Ejecutivo en El Ramo de Relaciones Exteriores: 1968–1969*. San Salvador: n.p., 1970.

Government of Honduras, Instituto de Investigaciones Económicas y Sociales. *Esboza de una Politica Agricola para Honduras*. Tegucigalpa: n.p., 1964.

———, Oficina Central de Información SECTIN. *El Conflicto de un Siglo*. Tegucigalpa: Comisión Publicitaria, 1976.

———, Oficina de Estudios Territoriales. *Fronteras de Honduras: Limites con Guatemala*. Tegucigala: Tipografía Nacional, 1930.

Grieb, Kenneth J. "The United States and the Rise of General Maximiliano Hernández Martínez," *Journal of Latin American Studies* 3 (1971): 151–72.

Henríquez, Orlando. *En el Cielo Escribieron Historia*. Tegucigalpa: Tipografía Nacional, 1972.

Herrera Cáceres, H. Roberto. *El Diferendo Hondureño-Salvadoreño: Su Evolución y Perspectivas*. Tegucigalpa: Imprenta Censa, 1977.

Huezo Selva, Rafael. *El Espacio Económico mas Singular del Continente Americano*. Santa Ana, El Salvador: Impreso Tipografico Comercial, 1972.

Jiménez, Eddy E. *La Guerra No Fue de Fútbol*. La Habana: Casa de las Americas, 1974.

Kantor, Harry, ed. *Patterns of Politics and Political Systems in Latin America*. Chicago: Rand McNally, 1969.

Karnes, Thomas L. *The Failure of Union: Central America 1824–1960*. Chapel Hill: University of North Carolina Press, 1961.

———. *Tropical Enterprise: Standard Fruit and Steam Ship Company in Latin America*. Baton Rouge: Louisiana State University Press, 1978.

Kepner, Charles David, Jr. *Social Aspects of the Banana Industry*. New York: AMS Press, 1967.

Latin American Bureau. *Violence and Fraud in El Salvador*. Longon: Latin American Bureau, n.d.

Leiva Vivas, Rafael. *Honduras: Fuerzas Armadas, Dependencia o Desarrollo*. Tegucigalpa: n.p., 1973.

———. *Un País en Honduras*. Tegucigalpa: Imprenta Calderón, 1969.

Bibliography

————. *Los Tratados Internacionales de Honduras*. Tegucigalpa: Universidad Nacional Autónoma de Honduras, 1971.

Lieuwen, Edwin. *Generals versus Presidents*. New York: Praeger, 1964.

López Arellano, Oswaldo. *Plan Nacional de Desarrollo: Conceptos Fundamentales*. Tegucigalpa: Instituto Nacional Agrario, 1974.

Lovo Castelar, Luis. "La Distribución y Tenencia de la Tierra en El Salvador." *La Universidad* 92 (1967): 107–15.

————. *La Guardia Nacional en Campaña: Relatos y Crónicas de Honduras*. San Salvador: Editorial Lea, 1971.

Luna, David Alejandro. *Manual de Historia Económica de El Salvador*. San Salvador: Editorial Universitaria, 1971.

McCann, Thomas P. *An American Company: The Tragedy of United Fruit*. New York: Crown Publishers, 1976.

McClelland, Donald H. *The Central American Common Market: Economic Policies, Economic Growth and Choices for the Future*. New York: Praeger, 1972.

McDonald, Ronald H. "Electoral Behavior and Political Development in El Salvador." *Journal of Politics* 31 (1969): 397–419.

Mallin, Jay. "Salvador-Honduras War, 1969: The 'Soccer War.' " *Air University Review* 21 (1970): 87–92.

Mariñas Otero, Luis. *Honduras*. Madrid: Ediciones Cultura Hispánica, 1963.

Martin, Percy Falcke. *Salvador of the Twentieth Century*. London: E. Arnold, 1911.

Martz, John D. *Central America: the Crisis and the Challenge*. Chapel Hill: University of North Carolina Press, 1959.

Martz, Mary Jane Reid. *The Central American Soccer War: Historical Patterns and Internal Dynamics of OAS Settlement Procedures*. Athens: Ohio University Center for International Studies, 1978.

————. "OAS Settlement Procedures and the El Salvador-Honduras Conflict." *South Eastern Latin Americanist* 19 (1975): 1–7.

May, Stacy, and Plaza Lasso, Galo. *The United Fruit Company in Latin America*. Washington: National Planning Association, 1958.

Mayorga Quirós, Román. "La Presión Demográfica en El Salvador: Las Trampas Neomalthusianas y la Teroia de la Reventazón. *Estudios Centroamericanos* 29 (1974): 603–38.

Mestas, Alberto de. *El Salvador: Pais de Lagos y Volcanos*. Madrid: n.p., 1950.

Meza Gallont, Rafael. *El Ejército de El Salvador: Breve Boceto Historico*. San Salvador: n.p., 1964.

Molina Chocano, Guillermo. *Estado Liberal y Desarrollo Capitalista en Honduras*. Tegucigalpa: Banco Central de Honduras, 1976.

Moran, Ed (pseud. of John McAward). "Human Rights for Peasants: The Roots of Violence in El Salvador. *Commonweal*, 13 October 1978, pp. 659–62.

Bibliography

Mundigo, Axel Ivan. *Elites, Economic Development and Population in Honduras.* Ithaca, N.Y.: Cornell University Press, 1972.

Nugent, Jeffery B. *Economic Integration in Central America: Empirical Investigations.* Baltimore: Johns Hopkins Press, 1974.

Organization of American States, Comisión Interamericana de Derechos Humanos. *Informe sobre la Situación de los Derechos Humanos en El Salvador.* Washington, D.C.: Organization of American States, 1978.

Osborne, Lilly de Jongh. *Four Keys to El Salvador.* New York: Funk, 1965.

Parada, Alfredo. *El Proceso de la Agresividad Hondureña.* San Salvador: Editoria Ahora, 1974.

Paredes, Lucas. *Liberalism y Nacionalismo: Trasnfuguismo Político.* Tegucigalpa: Imprenta Honduras, 1963.

Parker, Franklin D. *The Central American Republics.* London: Royal Institute of International Affairs, 1964.

————. "The Fútbol Conflict and Central American Unity." *Annals of the Southeastern Conference on Latin American Studies* 3 (1972): 44–59.

Parsons, Kenneth H. "Agrarian Reform in Southern Honduras." *Land Tenure Center Newsletter* no. 50 (1975): 6–14.

Pérez Brignoli, Héctor. *La Reforma Liberal en Honduras.* Tegucigalpa: Editorial Nuevo Continente, 1973.

Pinto Mejía, Edmundo. *Así Es Honduras.* Tegucigalpa: n.p., 1973.

Pippin, Larry L. "Soccer War or Demographic Conflict?" *The Pacific Historian* 14 (1970): 15–21.

Poblete Troncoso, Moisés, and Burnett, Ben G. *The Rise of the Latin American Labor Movement.* New Haven, Conn.: Yale University Press, 1960.

Poppino, Rollie E. *International Communism in Latin America: A History of the Movement.* New York: Free Press, 1964.

Posas Amador, M. "El Movimiento Obrero Hondureño: La Huelga de 154 y Sus Consecuencias." *Estudios Sociales Centroamericanos* 15 (1976): 93–127.

Prats, Raymond. *Genese et Evolution du Marche Common Centramericain.* Paris: La Documentation Française, 1971.

Ramírez, Asdrúbal. *Los Militares Patriotas y la Revolución Hondureña.* Tegucigalpa: Imprenta Calderón, 1972.

Reynolds, David R. *Rapid Development in Small Economies: The Example of El Salvador.* New York: Praeger, 1967.

Rodríguez, Mario. *Central America.* Englewood Cliffs, N.J.: Prentice Hall, 1965.

Rodríguez Beteta, Virgilio. *No Es Guerra de Hermanos sino de Bananos: Como Evité la Querra en Centroamerica en 1928.* Guatemala: Universidad de San Carols, 1969.

Bibliography

Rouquié, Alain. "Honduras - El Salvador, la Guerre de Cent Heures: Un Cas de 'Désintégration Régionale.' " *Revue Française de Science Politique* 21 (1971): 1290–1316.

Saavedra, David. *Bananos, Oro y Plata.* Tegucigalpa: Tipográficos Nacionales, 1935.

Saravia, Mario. *Fuerzas en Marcha.* San Salvador: n.p., 1949.

Secretario Permanente del Tratado General de Integración Económica Centroamericana. *El Desarrollo Integrado de Centroamerica en la Presente Década: Bases y Propuestas para el Perfeccionamiento y la Reestructación del Mercado Común Centroamericana.* Guatemala: SIECA, 1972.

Selva, Mauricio de la. "El Salvador: Tres Decades de Lucha." *Cuadernos Americanos* 21 (1962): 196–220.

Smith, T. Lynn. "Notes on the Population and Rural Social Organization in El Salvador." *Rural Sociology* 10 (1945): 359–79.

Stokes, William S. *Honduras: A Case Study in Government.* Madison: University of Wisconsin Press, 1950.

———. "The Land Laws of Honduras." *Agricultural History* 21 (1947): 148–54.

Stycos, J. Mayone, and Capa, Cornell. *Margin of Life: Population and Poverty in the Americas.* New York: Grossman, 1974.

Valades, Edmundo. *Los Contratos del Diablo: Las Concesiones Bananeras en Honduras y Centroamerica.* Mexico, D.F.: Editores Asociados, 1975.

Vallejo, Antonio R. *Límites de Honduras con El Salvador.* Tegucigalpa: Ediciones Nacionales, 1926.

Valásquez, César Vicente. *El Dilema Centroamericano.* Quito: Editorial Casa de la Cultura Equadoriana, 1974.

Valásquez Díaz, Maximiliano. *La Aplicación del Tratado de Río y la Agresión a Honduras.* Tegucigalpa: Universidad Nacional Autónoma de Honduras, 1969.

———. *Las Cuestiones Pendientes entre Honduras y El Salvador.* Tegucigalpa: n.p., 1976.

Vieytez, A. "La Emigración Salvadoreña a Honduras. *Estudios Centroamericanos* 24 (1969): 399–406.

Villanueva, Benjamín. "The Role of Institutional Innovations in the Economic Development of Honduras." *Land Tenure Center Newsletter* no. 34 (1968).

Webre, Stephen. *José Napoleón Duarte and the Christian Democratic Party in Salvadoran Politics: 1960–1972.* Baton Rouge: Louisiana State University Press, 1979.

White, Alastair. *El Salvador.* New York: Praeger, 1973.

Woodward, Ralph Lee, Jr. *Central America: A Nation Divided.* New York: Oxford University Press, 1976.

Wynia, Gary W. *Politics and Planners: Economic Development Policy in Central America.* Madison: University of Wisconsin Press, 1972.

Bibliography

DISSERTATIONS

Croner, Charles Marc. "Spatial Characteristics of Internal Migration to San Pedro Sula, Honduras." Michigan State University, 1972.

Daugherty, H. E. "Man-Induced Ecologic Change in El Salvador." University of California at Los Angeles, 1969.

Elam, Robert Varney. "Appeal to Arms: The Army and Politics in El Salvador, 1931–1964." University of New Mexico, 1968.

Fonck, Carlos O'Brien. "Modernity and Public Policies in the Context of the Peasant Sector in Honduras." Cornell University, 1972.

Harrison, Sandas Lorenzo. "The Role of El Salvador in the Drive for Unity in Central America." Indiana University, 1963.

Martinson, Tommy Lee. "Selected Changes in Agricultural Production and Economic Rent along the Western Highway in Honduras: 1952–1965." University of Kansas, 1970.

Mundigo, Axel Ivan. "Elites, Economic Development and Population in Honduras." Cornell University, 1972.

Villanueva, Benjamín. "Institutional Innovations and Economic Development: Honduras, a Case Study." University of Wisconsin, 1968.

Wilson, Everett A. "The Crisis of National Integration in El Salvador: 1919–1935." Stanford University, 1970.

NEWSPAPERS

El Salvador:
    La Crónica del Pueblo
    Diario de Hoy
    Diario Latino
    El Mundo
    La Prensa Gráfica
Honduras:
    El Cronista
    La Prensa
    El Pueblo
    El Tiempo
    La Tribuna Gráfica
United States Newspapers and Periodicals:
    Miami Herald
    Newsweek
    New York Times
    El Pulgarcito (San Francisco)
    El Salvador Reports (New York)
    Time
    Washington Post
Other:
    Central American Report (Guatemala)
    Latin America (Latin American Political Report) (London)

Bibliography

DOCUMENTS IN FOREIGN MINISTRY FILES

El Salvador:

"Copias de Declaraciones Autenticadas Vendidas por los Expulsa dos de la Republica de Honduras"

"Correspondencia General Recibida: Conflicto Honduras-El Salvador"

"Informe sobre la Misión Cumplida por El Embajador Jorege Fernandez y Richard A. Poole en El Salvador y Honduras entre los Dias 8 y 14 de Noviembre de 1969.

Honduras:

"Correspondencia Despachado Mayo-Junio, 1969"

"Expediente Confidencial sobre Incidente Ocurido el 25 Day de 1967 en la Hacienda de Dolores, Departamento de La Paz, Republica de Honduras."

"Tomo de Cable y Radios Nacionales, Enero a Diciembre, 1969."

(plus many uncollected documents)

INTERVIEWS

(More than a hundred persons were consulted; only the most important interviews are listed here):

César A. Batres: former foreign minister and frequent cabinet member in Honduras.

Policarpo Callejas: for many years deputy foreign minister of Honduras.

Ricardo Guillermo Castaneda: Salvadorean lawyer.

Arturo Castrillo Hidalgo: director-general of Regional Integration Foreign Ministry of El Salvador.

Fidel Chávez Mena: Salvadorean lawyer, leader of PDC.

Héctor Dada: professor at Universidad Centroamericana, San Salvador, later foreign minister.

Jorge Fidel Durón: former minister of foreign affairs of Honduras, historian.

Col. Joaquín Evelio Flores Amaya: Salvadorean army officer.

Col. Rafael Flores Lima: minister of information, El Salvador.

Virgilio Gálvez: member of Electoral Commission, ex-ambassador to El Salvador of Honduras.

José Napoleón González: Salvadorean newspaper publisher.

Francisco José Guerrero: Former foreign minister of El Salvador.

William Harbin: U.S. labor attaché, Tegucigalpa.

Baltasar Llort Escalante: former head of Salvadorean Red Cross.

Maria de Los Angeles: Department of Social Science, Universidad Nacional Autónomo de Honduras.

Nicolás Mariscal: Salvadorean priest-scholar.

Román Mayorga Quirós: rector of Universidad Centramericana, San Salvador, later junta member.

Gen. José Alberto Medrano: former head of the Salvadorean Guardia Nacional.

José María Méndez: writer, member of Salvadorean peace mission to Washington.

Herbert Mitchell: Former United States political affairs officer, San Salvador.

René Padilla Velasco: official of the Salvadorean Foreign Ministry.

Lt. Antonio Palacios: late officer of the Salvadorean army.

Pablo Pineda Madrid: chief of secretariate of territorial studies, Foreign Ministry of Honduras.

Oscar Reyes Bacca: Department of Journalism, Universidad Nacional Autónoma de Honduras, and official of the secretary of culture.

Ernesto Rivas Gallont: Salvadorean businessman, former Red Cross head.

José Antonio Rodríguez Porth: former foreign minister of El Salvador.

Msgr. Oscar Romero y Galdames: archbishop of San Salvador.

Gen. Fidel Sánchez Hernández: former president of El Salvador.

Colonel Roberto Santavañas: chief of intelligence, Salvadorean Army.

Paul Vinelli: Honduran banker.

William Walker: former United States political affairs officer, San Salvador.

Guillermo Ungo: secretary-general of MNR, later junta member in El Salvador.

Rosanna Zambrano: Honduran historian.

Index

DOMESTIC POLITICAL

MILITARY
CHURCH
HACIENDA   NEED $
UNIVERSITY

EXTERNAL POLITICAL PRESSURE

HAVE $ MULTINATIONALS
          FORGIAN GOVERNMENTS

          |
         ±F (only)
          |
PEASANT CONTROL

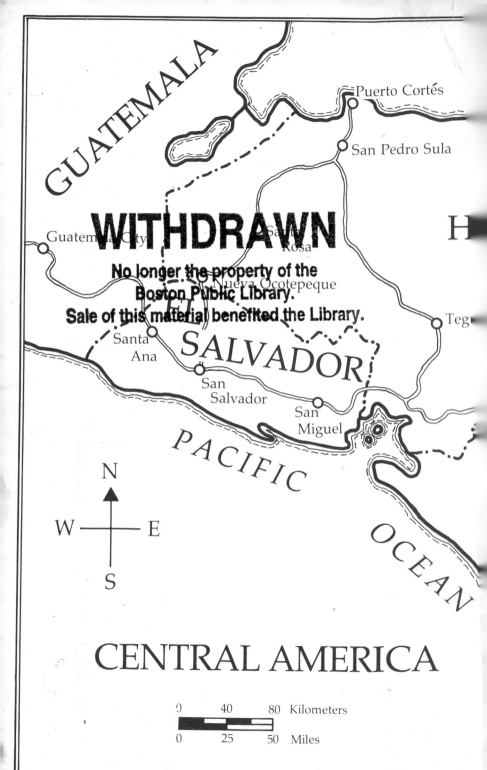

GUATEMALA

Puerto Cortés

San Pedro Sula

H

Guatemala City

Santa
Rosa

Nueva Ocotepeque

Teg

Santa
Ana

SALVADOR

San Salvador

San
Miguel

PACIFIC

N

W ——— E

S

OCEAN

CENTRAL AMERICA

9	40	80	Kilometers
0	25	50	Miles